Managing the
Adolescent
Classroom

In memory of my father—
A man who loved to tell stories

Managing the Adolescent Classroom

Lessons From Outstanding Teachers

GLENDA BEAMON CRAWFORD

Foreword by Thomas O. Erb

CORWIN PRESS
A Sage Publications Company
Thousand Oaks, California

For information:

Corwin Press
A Sage Publications Company
2455 Teller Road
Thousand Oaks, California 91320
www.corwinpress.com

Sage Publications Ltd.
1 Oliver's Yard
55 City Road
London EC1Y 1SP
United Kingdom

Sage Publications India Pvt. Ltd.
B-42, Panchsheel Enclave
Post Box 4109
New Delhi 110 017 India

Printed in the United States of America

Library of Congress Cataloging-in-Publication Data

Crawford, Glenda Beamon.
Managing the adolescent classroom: Lessons from outstanding teachers / Glenda Beamon Crawford.
    p. cm.
Includes bibliographical references and index.
ISBN 0–7619–3106–6 (cloth)—ISBN 0–7619–3107–4 (pbk.)
  1. Classroom management. 2. Teenagers—Education. I. Title.
LB3013.C73 2004
373.1102′4—dc22

2003027074

04 05 06 07 10 9 8 7 6 5 4 3 2 1

Acquisitions Editor:	Jean Ward
Production Editor:	Melanie Birdsall
Copy Editor:	Barbara Coster
Typesetter:	C&M Digitals (P) Ltd.
Proofreader:	Cheryl Rivard
Indexer:	Sylvia Coates
Cover Designer:	Michael Dubowe
Graphic Designer:	Lisa Miller

Contents

List of Figures

Foreword

The management of adolescents in classrooms is not just about following the rules of correct behavior for either students or teachers. Instead, classroom management is about the skillful application of several different principles to create positive learning environments.

A successful teacher has significant control over several factors that result in a well-managed classroom. The first of these factors is relationships—relationships between teachers and students and those fostered among students. The second is having a relevant, appropriate curriculum to teach. The third is providing engaging lessons for learners that contain an appropriate level of cognitive challenge in psychologically safe surroundings. All of these interact in a physical space that the teacher has power to affect. Finally, management is about helping students take personal responsibility for their learning and being held accountable for that learning.

Since classroom management is about a complex interaction of all these factors, the best way to learn about it is by observing successful managers at work and analyzing the elements contributing to their success. Glenda Beamon Crawford's *Managing the Adolescent Classroom* helps us do just that by providing a rich variety of case studies depicting successful classroom managers in action. This book offers a thorough guide for preservice, neophyte, and veteran teachers, as well as for those who supervise them, on how to establish truly well-managed classrooms.

Thomas O. Erb
Editor, *Middle School Journal*
Professor, University of Kansas

Acknowledgments

This book would not have been possible without the interest, commitment, and support of many special individuals. To each of these persons, I offer deep appreciation.

To Emily Dreyer, my research assistant, who traveled with me across the region in the cool darkness of fall mornings. Her observations and insights were invaluable in the book's creation and in her own preparation as a teacher of young adolescents.

To the outstanding middle level teachers who willingly opened the doors and worlds of their classrooms. This book celebrates their love of young adolescents and their joy in teaching them.

To the administrators whose instructional leadership and understanding of young adolescents set the right context for positive classroom management. They believe in the goodness and potential of these students and trust their teachers to teach them well.

To Jean Ward, senior acquisitions editor at Corwin Press. Her friendship and continuing encouragement of my professional endeavors are sincerely valued.

To Beth, Kenneth, April, and young Austin, who shared in the eventful summer.

To my mother, Polly, whose support has been constant.

To my sons, Michael and Brent, and new "daughter," Dodi. They are my most spirited and faithful advocates.

To Larry, my husband, who remained patient through the long hours of my writing. His unwavering love and pride never fail to humble me.

To Claude C. Ward, my special father, who was not ready to leave. He would have loved these stories.

Corwin Press would like to thank the following reviewers for their contributions:

Judith Irvin
Professor
College of Education
Florida State University
Tallahassee, Florida

Kristen Nelson
Director, Special Projects
Capistrano Unified School District
Orange County, California

Chris Stevenson
Professor Emeritus
Department of Education
University of Vermont
Burlington, Vermont

About the Author

 **Glenda Beamon Crawford's** experiences with young adolescent learners span nearly thirty years. She has taught Grades 4 through 12 and currently coordinates the Middle Grades Program at Elon University, where she is a professor of teacher education. She has authored two books, *Sparking the Thinking of Students, Ages 10–14* and *Teaching With Adolescent Learning in Mind,* and published several articles on structuring classrooms for young adolescent thinking and learning. She consults and presents regularly at state, national, and international conferences. Her research and teaching honors include the 2002 North Carolina Award for Outstanding Contribution to Gifted Education.

Introduction
and Overview

At McDougle Middle School, eighth grade students were sprawled out in clusters on the tile floor watching small windup toys wobble in forward movement alongside the length of a yardstick. High-volume chatter and relaxed laughter rose above the scene. The young teacher perched on her knees beside a group of students on the far side of the room.

Closer observation revealed that the students in Ms. Berge's class were conducting lab experiments to determine the negative acceleration rate of moving objects. The data that they collected and recorded were used for complex physics calculations, quite impressive mental activity for thirteen-year-olds! Thus began my quest to discover the procedures and secrets of teachers in adolescent classrooms who are recognized as outstanding classroom managers. Motivating this initiative was the key question, How do the best teachers of adolescents manage the physical, affective, and intellectual dimensions of classroom life in order for young adolescents to learn and develop socially, intellectually, and personally? The fourteen case studies that shape this book are the product of that year-long inquiry.

The purpose of this book is twofold. It first showcases classroom management strategies that work well for a group of exemplary teachers in Grades 5 through 9. More broadly, the book's purpose is to stimulate discussion about why these effectual approaches are developmentally appropriate for young adolescents, ages ten to fifteen. It is written for preservice and practicing teachers and other educators who are interested in learning about middle level teachers who manage the physical, social-emotional, and academic dimensions of the classroom environment to facilitate learning and responsible behavior.

DEFINING CLASSROOM MANAGEMENT

Because the term *classroom management* once conjured up images of teacher dominance and student acquiescence, it is important to clarify the way in which the concept is viewed in these case studies. Classroom management in the book's context includes three interrelated dimensions of the learning environment.

1. The first component is the physical, or the teacher's use of time, space, and structural environment.

2. The second is the affective element, or those strategies used to promote positive personal and interpersonal development.

3. A third dimension of classroom management is the cognitive element, or the teacher's use of intellectual engagement to motivate students' appropriate behavioral management and commitment to learning.

Classroom management thus embraces all that middle level teachers do to organize space, time, resources, and instructional experiences in support of learning.

The close association of classroom management and effective teaching is supported in the current literature (Emmer, Evertson, & Worsham, 2003; Good & Brophy, 2003; Marzano, 2003). Successful teachers are those who

- Intentionally and proactively organize the classroom environment;
- Communicate and maintain high expectations for behavior, social interaction, movement, and intellectual engagement;
- Seek to build positive relationships with students; and
- Promote student self-management.

They further have the wherewithal to observe and address potential problems with tact, fairness, and objectivity, a skill coined in earlier decades as *withitness* (Kounin, 1970).

This view of classroom management reflects a paradigm shift from a model of teacher control and student compliance to the creation of a learning community that promotes relationship, belonging, and achievement (Curwin & Mendler, 1988; Deci & Ryan, 1998; Wong & Wong, 1998). Within this learning environment, the teacher's expectations related to personal behavior management and academic engagement are clear, communicated, and consistently maintained. Integral also are the elements of order, safety, and discipline.

THE DEVELOPMENTAL PARADOX OF YOUNG ADOLESCENCE

Classroom management in the middle grades (5 through 9) must take into consideration the unique developmental nature of students whose bodies and minds are undergoing remarkable changes (Beamon, 1997, 2001). Shifts in metabolism can render young adolescents listless or trigger squirmy behavior, and often their physical endurance decreases. Rapid growth may cause their bones and joints literally to hurt (Van Hoose, Strahan, & L'Esperance, 2001). Highly desired social relationships can be charted on an erratic graph of joy and disappointment as friendship groups shape and reconfigure. As young adolescents' bodies begin to develop, they often puzzle over new feelings and sensations, and their interest in the opposite sex can simultaneously excite and bewilder. Emerging intellectual abilities also carry the capacity for abstract thinking and reasoning, yet these cognitive changes are accompanied by a complicating capacity for worry and self-consciousness.

These paradoxical developmental changes have considerable implication for classroom management at the middle level. Unlike younger students who need closer supervision and guidance or older students who are more independent and self-directed, young adolescents thrive in a learning environment that is typified simultaneously by structure and freedom. They need to be able to move physically and to talk and interact socially, yet they also must know that their behaviors and attitudes can help or impede classroom learning. They need routines, procedures, and expectations in order to learn to work collaboratively and productively. While young adolescents need academic challenge for cognitive growth, they also need support to make new learning connections and to acquire personal learning strategies. Effective classroom management at this level is thus characterized by an intentional regard for young adolescents' unique physical, social, personal, and intellectual needs.

The teachers in the following chapters appear to understand young adolescents' unique developmental needs and manage their classrooms responsively. Their instruction is intellectually engaging, socially interactive, and physically active. They allow their students choices, options, and multiple ways to approach and demonstrate learning. They provide support but continually focus on engendering efficacious responsibility for appropriate behavior and academic commitment. They create supportive, expectant, and challenging classrooms where young adolescents learn to think critically and ethically, and to respect and care about each other.

THE TEACHERS AND THEIR SCHOOLS

The fifteen teachers were selected for the case studies by criteria related to the physical, affective, and cognitive dimensions of classroom management. These factors included minimal observed or reported student behavior problems; maximum use of class time for academic study; high level of engagement of students in learning experiences; and elements of organization, safety, and respect with the classroom environment. The teachers were further recognized by administrators and colleagues for the ability to facilitate a learning environment that is responsive to young adolescent development.

The teachers represent six schools in four districts in the central Piedmont region of North Carolina. A discussion of the schools' demographics, philosophical context, and leadership style follows in Chapter 8. Collectively, the classrooms span Grades 5 through 9 and comprise a variety of content areas, which include traditional core subjects (science, social studies, language arts/literature, and mathematics) and the electives of art, health, physical education, and life skills (see Resource C for teacher profiles). The teachers differ in gender, race, licensure areas, level and kind of educational degrees, and years of experience, and their students include a wide range of academic levels and behavioral needs.

It is important to note that many of the teachers chosen for this study have certification and teaching experience that extend from young adolescence through upper secondary school, so while the focus of this book is on classroom management for students in the developmental hinge years of Grades 5 to 9, the management models and practices that these teachers present have applicability for upper high school students as well.

It is also important to note that the participants in Grades 6 through 8, who teach the core subject areas of language arts, social studies, mathematics, and science, are members of interdisciplinary teams. The benefit of middle level teams in promoting supportive communities for young adolescent learning and personal development is widely recognized in the literature (Jackson & Davis, 2000; Stevenson, 1998; Van Hoose et al., 2001). By promoting interpersonal connections, increasing opportunities for academic success, and enabling a more cohesive context for common goals and expectations, team organization is recognized as a conducive structure for effective classroom management (Stevenson, 1998, pp. 218–19). Although the case studies predominantly focus on individual classroom management experiences, one titled "It Takes Two" in Chapter 7 showcases the collaborative benefits of a two-teacher seventh grade interdisciplinary team.

SHAPING THEIR STORIES

For two semesters, in early morning or later in the day between our classes, Emily Dreyer, my student research assistant, and I visited the teachers' classrooms. Our purpose was to learn all we could about their classroom management approaches. Onsite, Emily and I scripted copious notes related to the physical, affective, and cognitive dimensions of classroom life. We documented the teachers' instructional presentation and interpersonal interactions with their students, and snapped numerous photos of the physical outlay of their classrooms. Follow-up included informal conversations with the teachers and their principals, colleagues, and students, e-mails, formal questionnaires, and interviews with the teachers to verify our findings. Each teacher also shared pertinent materials and kept a running journal of strategies they found to be workable.

Initially, Emily and I were struck by the variations in the way each teacher uniquely coordinated the physical environment, interacted with students, and conducted instruction. A multifaceted color-coded organizational system in one classroom, for example, contrasted sharply with the cluttered room and free-flowing interaction in another. Other differences from one teacher to another included tolerance for noise level, the structural layout of the classroom, and the daily procedures related to movement and instruction.

As our observations and contact continued, however, Emily and I were able to discern patterns or themes that appeared to cut across grade levels or content areas. Each theme is noticeable to some degree in all of the teachers' classroom management approaches, but each pattern is more characteristically dominant in fewer. The arrangement of the fourteen case studies into titled chapters purposefully highlights these connecting and prevalent themes. The brief synopses below and the introduction of each chapter provide a rationale for this organization. The culminating Chapter 9 provides a discussion of the thematic commonalities and draws a parallel to current research in classroom management and in developmentally appropriate middle level practice.

It is also important and interesting to note that within each chapter's thematic organization are variations in the way this theme manifests in the case study. The theme of "high expectations and instructional accommodation" is prevalent in Chapter 3, for example, yet the individual management style of each of the three eighth grade language arts teacher contrasts sharply. Shifting responsibility to students is the connecting pattern of the two case studies in Chapter 4; however, differences are apparent in grade level, kind of student accountability, and nature of classroom environment. Accompanying many of the case studies are favorite strategies shared by the teachers, and at the end of each chapter are questions to facilitate discussion and analysis with suggested responses.

THEMATIC ORGANIZATION OF CHAPTERS

Chapter 2, titled "Management Through High Engagement," showcases two teachers who set high expectations for student learning and behavior and expect no less. Academic engagement is high and rules are simple: Learning is going on here. Don't impede the progress! In Case Study 1, "Just Don't Get in the Way of My Learning!" a seventh grade science teacher near a large university community manages through high-paced academic engagement. A simple test review becomes a shared intellectual task of generating, synthesizing, and evaluating content knowledge related to genetics and cell division. Case Study 2, Assessment-Driven Management, reveals the way an eighth grade language arts teacher uses a computer-based assessment system to identify students' learning needs and to determine the composition and flexible rotation plan for groups.

Chapter 3, "Shifting Speed—Not Lowering Expectations," is a trilogy of case studies that feature language arts teachers who have back-to-back classes of advanced learning and inclusion. While their personal management styles differ, each teacher holds high expectations for student learning regardless of academic level. In Case Study 3, A *Silent* Seminar?? eighth grade academically gifted students move like clockwork through the transitions of multifaceted lessons about theme and literary perspective. On another day this same teacher reviews for a test with an inclusion class by simulating the game of Jeopardy. Interestingly, the 500-level slots in each literary category are many of the first chosen!

Case Study 4, "She Never Stops Teaching," profiles a sixth grade language arts teacher who does not allow the students' diverse ability levels to prevent her from using an instructional approach she knows is a good one. An advanced class is divided into literature circles, each becoming "expert" in one of four young adolescent novels they have self-selected. The fact that her second block is an inclusion class with a range of special needs doesn't stop her from using a variation of the same cooperative learning strategy. In Case Study 5, "I Try Not to Fight Every Battle," the teacher's approach is noticeably realistic. Ten of the nineteen students in this eighth grade inclusion class are identified as exceptional, another by Section 501, and several have attention deficit disorders (ADDs). Rather than lowering expectations, he opens the opportunity for all students to complete a multifaceted research project, with amazing success!

In Chapter 4, "Shifting Responsibility to Students," the teachers place prime emphasis on students' assuming responsibility for classroom administration, behavior management, and their own learning. Case Study 6, Class Secretary, features an eighth grade teacher who relies on designated students, selected for a week's duration, to maintain a notebook for attendance records, homework assignments, and missed work. It is also their responsibility to ensure that the absent student signs off! The Land of Woz is the title of Case Study 7. The fifth grade teacher firmly believes that students need to take charge of their learning. The ten-year-old Wizards serve as tour guides for third and fourth graders along the school's nature trail on Earth Day. They also roll cages and glass containers of the classroom "critters" on carts to other classes to share their expertise on reptiles, mammals, and amphibians.

The prevalent theme in Chapter 5, "Making the Physical Environment a Partner," is the teachers' strategic use of the physical environment to facilitate student movement and learning. In this scenario in Case Study 8, "This Is Their Space . . . Not My Room," an orderly system of work folders, designated student assistants, labeled shelves and cabinets, multiple designs and models, and ample supplies enables this art classroom to seemingly run itself. Color drives the organizational plan for the sixth grade mathematics class in Case Study 9, If It's Written in Blue. . . . Color-coded folders, board assignments, manipulative boxes, and portfolios ease the coordination of activity within and transition between the three schedule blocks.

The two teachers featured in Chapter 6, "Knowing What Works for You", differ in teaching style, personality, subject area, and years of experience. Each, however, knows what is necessary to facilitate learning and what they personally need from students to make this happen. In Case Study 10, Proceed With Caution, the complex nature of rotating center activity in a seventh grade life skills class justifies the time taken initially for an elaborate explanation of the room's physical environment. A heterogeneous group of seventh graders follow the teacher on a visual tour as they become acclimated to the procedures for using the kitchen, sewing, child care, and personal image centers. The personal style of the young eighth grade science teacher in Case Study 11, All Wound Up, offers a sharp contrast. The classroom and adjacent hallway are transformed into "labs" for collaborative experiments to determine the negative acceleration rate of a windup toy. This teacher tolerates considerable talking as small groups of students test, record, discuss, and figure complex calculations.

The power of the positive is the permeating theme in the last three case studies in Chapter 7, "Believing Less Is More and Positive Is Better." From sixth grade health education to ninth grade English literature, these student-centered classes are conducive environments for adolescent social-emotional development. Case Study 12, Battle of the Sexes, showcases a teacher in two settings: a sixth grade health classroom during a sex education unit and the school gymnasium, where she manages the rotating drills of a co-ed group of forty-eight seventh graders. Emphasis in both locations is placed on adolescents' positive emotional and social development as the frame of reference for actions, thinking, and lifestyle. The two seventh grade teachers in Case Study 13, Divide and Conquer, are a true team. Each is responsible for a specialty area, either language arts or math, and they team on a rotating two-week schedule to teach science and social studies. What is unique is that they group students flexibly according to individual needs, interests—and even, on occasion, by gender!

The ninth grade teacher in the last case study (14), They Call Her "Miss D," has taught high school English for seven years. A focal point of her classroom is the No Putdown Zone, an area on a small front bulletin board. Covered in student-generated reminders of respectful language, it serves as a deterrent to negative comments often exchanged by fourteen-year-old students.

Chapter 8 provides information about the context and geographical setting of each of the five schools. Key administrators share personal philosophies related to young adolescent learning and outline school expectations and policies regarding classroom management. Chapter 9 culminates the book with additional analyses of the common themes connecting the case studies. Reference is drawn to underlying current research in young adolescent development, social cognitive theory, motivation, and learning.

CLASSROOM MANAGEMENT IN THE MIDDLE

I have written and spoken often about the kind of classroom that best supports the intellectual, physical, social, and personal needs of young adolescents, ages ten to fifteen. My belief that these environments should allow movement and interaction, and that instruction should be engaging, relevant, and appropriately challenging, is grounded in my own teaching, personal research, and the work of middle level educators. Young adolescents deserve an orderly, safe place to learn; they also need for their minds, emotions, and individualities to be stimulated within meaningful and achievable learning experiences. They respond positively to high expectations for accountability, clear communication of limitations, fair treatment, and consistency. In classrooms where young adolescents' needs are met and the focus is on building academic competence and personal responsibility, most behavioral problems are minimized.

Each teacher who so graciously opened the classroom door revealed a dynamic environment supportive of students' unique developmental needs. Interaction is intellectually engaging, expectations for student learning and actions are high and firm, and good behavior is prevalent. Classroom management at the middle level is the proactive and strategic structuring of the physical, affective, and cognitive dimensions of classroom life, with consideration for young adolescents and their learning.

This book offers many ideas rather than one formula for good classroom management. Each teacher is as unique as his or her personal style and preference. Through a collection of case studies and an analysis chapter, this book distinguishes some commonalities among outstanding classroom managers and explores why these identified practices are effective for young adolescent learning and development. In a time of unsettling public debate about the roles of school in society and the commitment of teachers—when the odds seem to be cast against good teachers and teaching—I have had the opportunity to learn about classroom management from a group of exemplary ones. The following pages share their stories.

2

Management Through High Engagement

Teachers in the following two case studies focus on learning, full speed ahead! Each views classroom management through the lens of high expectations for student academic engagement. Any action or behavior that interferes with the learning process is simply not acceptable or tolerated. They share the philosophy that "less is better" in the way of rules. In both instances, the only unwritten rule is not to interfere with anyone else's learning. According to these teachers, this rule covers them all.

Priscilla Dennison in Case Study 1 teaches seventh grade science at McDougle Middle School in a progressive school system near the University of North Carolina at Chapel Hill. McDougle Middle has been the test site for several collaborative research projects with the university. Ms. Dennison has been specifically involved in a successful strategy called "looping," in which a teacher follows classes from sixth to seventh grade before returning to sixth to begin again with another group.

Andrew Fox, an eighth grade language arts educator at Turrentine Middle School in the nearby Alamance-Burlington System, teaches in one of the mobile units added to accommodate the fast-growing student body. A former high school teacher and administrator who has recently moved into the Burlington area, he brings to his Turrentine classroom a keen understanding of standards-based assessment.

"JUST DON'T GET IN THE WAY OF MY LEARNING!"

Case Study 1

Step right up to the greatest show on earth! It's a brand-new game show called "Clarify the Mush," and I thought of it myself. On the board you see four key terms you need to understand from Chapter 3 on cell division: *Mendel, probability, meiosis,* and *DNA-RNA*. Let's check your "mush index." For a 10, these terms are so clear that you could write a textbook. You could win the Nobel Prize and share the money with your favorite science teacher. Unfortunately, a 1 means your mush is so thick and gooey that it's impenetrable. What's a zero? You must still be in bed!

Now, only you can clarify your own mush, so let's get the show started! You'll need a fresh clean sheet of notebook paper, not torn out, and preferably a pencil. Three-Two-One. Lights! Camera! Action! We're on the air. Let's try and leave here with less mush than before!

Thus begins Ms. Dennison's review for Monday's test on human genetics. She instructs the seventh graders to copy the four terms on their papers and to write a statement about what they know and understand about each. No books are allowed. After four minutes, she asks the students to draw a line under their work and rewrite the four terms. "Listen carefully," she cautions, "for the rules now change." For the second writing of the terms, the students are asked to work with a partner to combine their statements into a joint (better) one. "I know you like to talk!" Ms. Dennison interjects. The seventh graders are permitted to check their books for *one* (and only one) of the terms, if they so choose. "On your mark. Get set. Take it away," and the collaboration between partners starts.

During this second interval, Ms. Dennison moves briskly among the seven tables of four students each, giving pointers and reminders of the directions for the task. "I'm looking. You're looking. You're lookin' good! Remember, only one section. Be sure you both agree. Both people need to write down the joint statement. You should be on the second one by now. You are halfway through your time!" After six minutes, the students are asked again to draw a line under their work and record the terms for a third time.

"Look up so I'll know you're with me," Ms. Dennison cues. "The rules are changing." For the third set of terms, all four of the students at the table have the task of combining their ideas into a single group statement. Books are allowed but, as before, to look up only one of the terms. Ms. Dennison continues her monitoring, offering feedback and suggestions. "What does that mean, 'cut in half'? What's special about those chromosomes? Good. Good statement. Use your book if you are stuck. Remember, you are a team. You need to try and work together. One more minute!"

Six minutes later, Ms. Dennison directs the seventh graders' attention again to the front whiteboard. "We're going back to our studio audience. Are you ready? I need someone at a lucky table to share one statement. Other tables can add as we go. Start us out!" she calls, as she points to the "lucky" table. In round-robin fashion, one of the students at the table begins to share information while Ms. Dennison records key phrases from their statements on the board. Next to the term *Mendel* she writes, "monk/scientist, peas, understood genetics, dominant and recessive." She interjects, "Mendel was the main man. He was so good that he was given the nickname Father of Genetics. Ironic, don't you think, considering he was a monk?" A few of the young adolescents pick up on her humor and giggle. One girl turns to explain the meaning of the pun to her partner.

Ms. Dennison next asks a student in the front for a nickel. She tosses it into the air and slaps it on the back of her hand with the familiar query, "Heads or tails?" Three tosses later, when only heads have resulted, she ventures, "What if I said, 'It can't be heads again because it's already been heads three times'?" The twelve-year-olds are not to be stumped, and remind her that there is a 50 percent chance for each toss of the coin. "Do you mean it could be heads *again?* What if I flipped it 500 times?" Ms. Dennison tosses the coin again and returns it to the young owner. "Now that's the main idea of probability," she summarizes. The discussion continues to a higher level, however, with Ms. Dennison's next question: "Tell me now, How does the concept of probability relate to genetics?"

To illustrate for the seventh graders the connection between probability and genetics, Ms. Dennison sketches a diagram of a Punnett square on the whiteboard. "We're not talking about winning the lottery here but about genes," she kids. She asks a question about the probability of an offspring inheriting a particular trait, such as hair or eye color, and fills in one cell of the square. "Does that mean we cross that block off?" she probes. "I'm looking through the crowd for that one hand." A female student indicates "No." "You're right, but why?"

The interaction continues as the other key terms are discussed. To help students clarify the concept of meiosis, or genes passing from parents to offspring, Ms. Dennison contrasts the term with mitosis. "We're talking sex cells here—female ovum, male sperm," she explains. A few "Oohs" are heard from the girls. Ms. Dennison presses further: "What happens without the right number of chromosomes in mitosis?" When a student responds, "Mutation," she jokes, "Yes, like a two-headed cow—but you know, it might just be a smarter cow!"

Ms. Dennison reviews the concepts of DNA and RNA with this similar exchange of question, response, and demonstration. She refers back to earlier in the week when the students had constructed a model of a double helix. "Remember, DNA stands for deoxyribonucleic acid," she smiles. "Throw that word out at dinner tonight!"

As the forty-five-minute period ends, Ms. Dennison exclaims, "Wow, we did it!" She reminds the seventh graders to click the day's notes into notebooks, to look back over the chapter in the book, and to make a couple of flash cards. Flash cards as a study guide earn the young adolescents bonus points. "Click it in. Click it in. I want to hear clicks." As students stand to change classes (no bells at McDougle), Ms. Dennison asks for a "mush level count." From the show of hands, it is evident that the index has climbed to a more encouraging indication. The students exit and Ms. Dennison erases the board notes. Four minutes later, another class is seated and a new show begins.

Ms. Dennison has taught science at McDougle Middle School in the Chapel Hill-Carrboro Schools for the past ten years. Licensed in elementary education and sixth through eighth grade science, she holds a master's of education in science. One summer she traveled with fifteen youngsters for a six-week science study across the United States. She firmly believes that classrooms should be places of safe, productive learning and that it is the teacher's responsibility to create this environment. Through four classes of approximately twenty-eight students a day, she works energetically to maintain a focus on young adolescent learning.

Ms. Dennison's classroom is spacious and brightly lit with side windows overlooking a central brick patio. A variety of plants, including philodendron, cacti, and shamrock, and colorful betas swimming in the fish bowls line the wide windowsills. On one of the glass fish bowls is an Elvis sticker. Side and back counters are marked with small numbers to denote the periods of the day. Beneath these, a few students' cell construction projects wait to be claimed. Along the opposite side and back of the room are six large sinks. Above one of these sinks on a glassed-in cabinet are scattered the tempura paint handprints of some of Ms. Dennison's former students. The hall pass, a funky-looking orange flip-flop, is tucked in the door handle of another of these cabinets.

Pictures of cells line the wall above the whiteboard in the front of the classroom. On a side bulletin board, a poster reminds students that in thirty years, the materialistic concerns they have today will be of no consequence: What will matter, however, will be their learning and how they use it. Above the lab table in the center front is the ubiquitous reflection mirror found in many science classrooms. Ms. Dennison's desk, where she's rarely seen seated, is also centered at the front. Her denim jacket hangs over her chair.

One phenomenon in the physical environment of Ms. Dennison's classroom is that there are no posted rules. The nearest to a regulatory statement is a sign that bears the words "Don't shoot birds of prey." When asked about the noticeable absence of student rules and consequences, she responds that there is only one classroom rule: "Just don't get in the way of my learning." It's an expectation that holds for both student and teacher. She believes that much misbehavior is associated with bored kids who are not learning interesting material or who are trying to learn something they cannot access.

> She believes that much misbehavior is associated with bored kids who are not learning interesting material or who are trying to learn something they cannot access.

"Kids want to be seen as smart," she stresses. "You have to find the key to make a student's 'smart' find its way out." She continues, "I try to keep it fun. If needed, I am firm, but I get over it fast and move on. I try to erase the day before and start each day over as a new one."

Ms. Dennison does admit that she has personal preferences related to the management of classroom learning activity. Noise, such as the screeching of chairs, bothers her. Consequently, she has padded the ends of the students' chair legs with tennis balls. Perfumes give her a headache, and voice changes affect her in the same way as some people react to fingernails scraping across a chalkboard. "We talk about what bothers us in class and how we can deal with it. They realize that I am just a person with them and that it is *my* life in this classroom, too."

Ms. Dennison's understanding of young adolescents and their developmental needs is evident. She knows that her students are testing their limits and need to know boundaries, and that they can differ from one day to the next as they deal with hormones and personal issues. She believes that the consequences for students' actions must fit the kid and the behavior, and she is direct and honest about what are acceptable standards for their choices and actions. Ms. Dennison acknowledges that middle school students are in a rough period in their lives: Braces hurt their teeth, social acceptance and friendships concern them, and clothes are valued disproportionately. According to Ms. Dennison, young adolescents need opportunities to make choices related to academic learning and personal management, and she tries to provide these. The following scenario illustrates.

Assessment by Choice

The scene is one month later on a rainy morning in mid-October. It is assessment day for the genetics unit, and the students have been given the choice of one of two ways to be tested: a traditional unit test or a poster, due that day, that depicted the genealogy of four inherited family traits. The seventh graders could thus decide if they wanted to take the in-class written assessment or prepare a poster at home. Ms. Dennison is managing two sets of directions, one for the test group that will remain in the classroom and a second for the poster group that is transitioning into the hall corridor. She distributes the paper tests with these comments, "I'm here for questions. I'll be in and out of the room, so it may look like I'm not, but I am. If you get stuck, ask. I want you to understand the questions. Guess what! If you don't understand the questions, you probably won't get the answers. Stay focused."

Out in the hallway, "Trace Your Genes" posters are being hung on the metal strips for a peer review. This culminating assessment required the seventh graders to trace the four genetic traits in twelve individuals back through four generations of family. The final product was to be a poster-sized pedigree chart with a legend. The poster group had traced a range of family traits, including hair color, tongue rolling, nose shape, freckles, dimples, and handedness. Their legends incorporated symbols for adoption, divorce, death, even twins. All of the posters are colorful, and some have been enhanced with family photographs. The task description follows.

Trace That Gene!

1. Look at sheets we have used in class for ideas. Choose any four traits that are hereditary and could be traced in your family. They do not have to be your phenotype.

2. Interview family members to determine who has these traits. You must show twelve individuals and three generations.

3. Draw a pedigree chart as a rough draft for the poster. Remember that squares represent male members and circles represent females. Create a color key and fill in squares and circles to show traits.

4. Enlarge your chart to poster size (25" by 22"). Make it neat and colorful for display.

On this day, the students are responsible for grading their own posters and that of four peers using a 100-point scoring rubric (see Figure 2.1). "They are playing me today," Ms. Dennison remarks. Prior to beginning the peer review, however, each student in the poster group is required to complete, to Ms. Dennison's satisfaction, a short content review sheet in order to "certify" their eligibility to evaluate. Review sheets completed, the hallway becomes a bustle of activity as students move with their scoring rubrics from poster to poster.

Back in the room, Ms. Dennison begins to collect science books for the unit from students who have finished the test. A $15 fee is charged if any book is lost. She pleads with the students who have yet to claim their cell projects: "Friends, Romans, and countrymen. Pick up your cell! Put it in your hope chest, on your mantel, or decorate the Thanksgiving table." As the class time draws to an end, she reminds the twelve-year-olds that they will be starting a unit on weather the next day. "Don't mess with the lady who's starting to do weather or you might get zapped with lightning!" The students laugh and spill into the hall to go to their next class.

Just as the high expectations Ms. Dennison has for her students, she is herself focused on continual self-improvement as an educator. She willingly participates in a systemwide survey that is completed by students halfway through the academic year. Data, which reflect the students' perceptions of Ms. Dennison as a teacher, are for her and the principal's use only. The information gained enables Ms. Dennison to reflect on her instructional practices and responsibilities, and she takes this feedback seriously. Asked to share what she believes are her best classroom management strategies, she offers, "It's all about me—how I keep my cool and don't take anything personally, how I try to be funny, how I dislike the action and not the actor. I try to rebuild the kids positively after any negative exchange."

Ms. Dennison also acknowledges that she is fortunate to teach the same students for a two-year period. This looping pattern allows a teacher to move up a grade level with the same students, thus sixth to seventh, before moving back to the sixth grade level to begin the process with another group. She and some of her colleagues have participated in related research with professors in the school of education at the local university, and the results have been positive in promoting student self-efficacy and self-esteem. "I get to know my students well. I feel very benevolent to them. They are *my* kids." It is no wonder that high school students frequently return to Ms. Dennison's class to scribble "We miss you" messages on the whiteboard.

Figure 2.1 Assessment Rubric for Project

Trace That Gene!		
Review different posters and answer the following for each one.		

	Grading Scale	
Review different posters and answer the following for each one. _____ name on poster	On time	10 points _____
List the 4 traits they traced: _____ _____ _____ _____	Correct spelling	10 points _____
	Neatness, legibility, spacing, ink	10 points _____
Which trait shows the clearest pattern of heredity? _____	Valid traits and names	10 points _____
Which trait shows the least pattern of heredity? _____	Different color/syn for prototype	10 points _____
How many people did they use to trace the trait? _____	12 individuals/3 generations	10 points _____
Rate the following about the poster: 1 (low) to 10 (high).	Key, clear markings, genetic lines	10 points _____
Neatness _____ Spelling _____ Straight lines _____ Clear color marking _____ Symbols/key _____	Each generation on same plane	10 points _____
List the symbols you see used on the poster. _____	Name, title	10 points _____
_____ _____ _____	Total	100 points _____

SOURCE: Used with permission from P. Dennison, McDougle Middle School, Chapel Hill, NC.

ASSESSMENT-DRIVEN MANAGEMENT

Case Study 2

Andy Fox is proud of his folders. Orange folders are for first block, dark blue for second, and light blue for third. Red ones hold the loose-leaf paper that he provides for each student. His eighth graders find their personal folders stacked with the writing and literature book inside their desks in a designated order. Before leaving, they check the bright yellow "In Your Desk" poster at the front board to make sure the folders and books are back in correct order for the next block of eighth graders. Granted, the use of color-coded folders is a sensible and prevalently used organizational strategy for young adolescents' schoolwork. Mr. Fox's colored folders, however, serve a purpose beyond that of a holding file for his students' papers. Inside each is an intricate assessment system that he has designed to individualize and thus maximize student learning and self-regulation. This unique management system enables him to track the academic, behavioral, and social progress of the seventy-five thirteen-year-olds he teaches each day. The way this organizational scheme works for him is described below.

The mobile unit where Mr. Fox teaches at Turrentine Middle School in the Alamance-Burlington Schools is bustling with activity. The previous day, students had taken a diagramming practice quiz to assess their ability to identify subjects and predicates, and to identify and place adjectives, adverbs, and prepositional phrases within sentences. Results on this preassessment had varied significantly. Using a simple spreadsheet program, Mr. Fox had run a response item analysis to determine which skill areas the students possessed or needed to acquire. Through the calculation, he divided the eighth graders into three need-based groups and planned an appropriate task for each cluster.

When students arrived for today's class, they had found a colored strip of adhesive paper stuck inside their folders—the designation for their assigned group. Also inside the folders were each student's individual quizzes, scored and categorized by areas of skill need or skill mastery. Mr. Fox had given instructions for the eighth graders to join their group at a designated location in the room and begin work on their particular task. The students in Group A had showed a high proficiency range of approximately 80 to 100 percent on the previous day's assessment. Clearly needing a challenge beyond simple diagramming, the first group is working near the back of the mobile unit on this task: "Write a sentence that contains two prepositional phrases, one used as an adjective and one used as an adverb, and two adjectives other than *a, an,* or *the.*"

Group B, comprised of students scoring in the 60 to 80 percent range, has been asked to diagram two sample sentences for Mr. Fox to check. They are located near the front of the class. If their diagramming is correct, they will be given the OK to move to the back, join Group A, and begin generating their own sentences. The third group had scored below 60 percent and needed significant practice in diagramming. They are working near the whiteboard at the side of the room. For part of the time, Mr. Fox uses the whiteboard for a minireview lesson; at other times, he circulates from group to group. Near the end of the work period, all students, their attention focused on the front whiteboard, are able to diagram successfully a sentence containing all the adjective and adverbial components: "The giant boat from Greece sailed slowly to the island off the coast of Liberia." The real quiz will follow the next day, and Mr. Fox's students are better prepared.

When asked about this assessment-driven management system, Mr. Fox quickly confesses that his students *love* it. "The groups are flexible," he explains, "and shift according to what they need. As soon as they 'get it,' they can move to another group. There is no shame, because as soon as they demonstrate proficiency, they know they can go to a higher level where the work is more motivating." He follows this procedure regularly. After giving an assessment, he groups the thirteen-year-olds according to shared strengths and needs.

> The key to this instructional management system is individualization.

He conducts remedial lessons focused on problem areas for some and enrichment lessons for others. At times, he gives the same problem to all students and subdivides them so that he can approach the instruction in varying ways.

According to Mr. Fox, the key to this instructional management system is individualization. Inside each folder, in addition to daily class work and various assessments, is a record of the student's progress on nine-week grade-level competencies. He schedules a four- to five-minute conference with each student twice per week to review his or her personal growth. "No matter how low a student might be performing," Mr. Fox justifies, "you can always find a reference point to begin." The folder system gives him a solid basis for making educational decisions, and he believes that it keeps the students focused on improvement. In his class, the young adolescents seem to know where they are and where they're headed. They also can begin to take some ownership in their own learning management.

> Determine what's essential for them to learn and then how to reduce the complexity.

Though his approach might be referred to as management by numbers, Mr. Fox confesses that at times it could be called measurement by hunches. "I have to try to develop strategies that will *work* for each student," he maintains. "It's a continual refinement process, trying to determine what's essential for them to learn and then how to reduce the complexity."

The décor of Mr. Fox's mobile classroom is simple. No slick motivational posters or decorative bulletin boards are hung on the walls, and no student projects are on display. The space is small and the students are large. Two whiteboards cover most of the front and right side walls. A sizable laminated chart labeled "Pronouns" distinguishes subject and object forms from singular and plural possessive and indefinite. A bar stool where Mr. Fox perches to lead whole-class activities or to give directions is positioned behind a red podium in the front. His desk, the site for student conferences, sits kitty-cornered in the back right area of the unit, and his computer, always on, is to one side. Student desks are arranged in long and short rows; the size of the room allows no option for tables. A blue ballpoint pen lies in the pencil tray of each student's desk. Unlike many middle level classrooms, no lists of rules and consequences are posted.

A meticulous planner, Mr. Fox's typed lesson plans are carefully aligned with grade-level curricular competencies. Each plan includes instruction for the whole class and group designations and tasks that have been differentiated by his assessment of each student's academic and behavioral progress. The range of diverse learning needs, particularly in his two heterogeneous language arts blocks, makes these learning accommodations imperative.

On many days, Mr. Fox's individualized assessment of his eighth graders' progress does not involve number crunching. The entire class, for example, reads S. E. Hinton's (1967) *The Outsiders.* All students are expected to complete the book and write character analysis summaries that will be typed in the computer lab. Class time is allotted for oral and silent reading, discussion, writing, and word processing. Mr. Fox's lesson plan may denote that one group is "ahead on reading or finished," the second, "slightly behind on reading and summaries," and a third, "behaviorally behind and behind on all assignments." While the first and second groups are assigned the task to complete the novel reading and work on character descriptions, the students in the third group, Mr. Fox's plan indicates, "must get caught up on reading before continuing with character summaries." After lunch, in the second half of the block, the entire class will go to the computer lab to begin typing what they have written thus far.

Mr. Fox's systematic planning begins even before a period's lesson has ended. He jots notes to himself that indicate when a student moves to another group or that the class might need to read about twenty minutes to finish Chapter 1 on the following day. He also color codes his lesson plans to indicate what was planned and what actually happened during the course of the class. He might type special reminders to himself in contrasting colors, for example, related to an individual student's problem with prepositional identification so he will be certain to check the student's progress that day.

Postlesson comments are also added so Mr. Fox can keep up with class interactions. One of his reflection notes specified, for instance,

> Only got to read a little but went over the characters again and talked about point of view. The class identified Ponyboy as the narrator. I posed this question for them to think about: "How do you describe a character who is the narrator of the story? Where do you get your information from?"

On another day he wrote,

> I was really happy to note that this went according to plan. All groups went right along. . . . By the end of the period, the whole class was back in the same place and up to speed. I really like the format for this.

Mr. Fox justifies these notes: "It will help with next year's planning."

Mr. Fox's classroom management by assessment, flexible grouping, and high-energy organization and planning is accompanied by no-nonsense expectations for student behavior. As he moves in and around the desks, responding to raised hands, he seems to have the proverbial eye in the back of his head. He directs a warning to a student across the room: "If I were to come over there, would you be working?" To another student, he indicates, "It's been eight or nine minutes since I left you. I see no progress." When it is time for lunch, he reminds students that they know the procedure for lining up in this way: "Ladies and gentlemen, remember the trip that never happened to the library? Remember the trip to the computer lab that never happened?" He does not, nor does he need to, raise his voice.

Though no rules are visible, Mr. Fox's expectations are apparent in the way he and the eighth graders interact. When the door of the unit opens and a girl enters and goes to her seat, Mr. Fox, without turning his body fully in her direction, tells her matter-of-factly to exit. She does, comes back in, and says, "Excuse me," before she sits again. At another point, he asks a disruptive student to tell him the Number 1 rule. The boy responds, "To mind my own business." When asked about his classroom expectations, Mr. Fox explains that the one unwritten rule, which the students know, is not to do anything that disrupts someone else's learning. "When applied," he attests, "it covers every situation."

Mr. Fox's behavior management approach could be described as a mixture of firmness, humor, and proximity. He teaches one block of academically gifted students and two blocks that contain a wide range of learning needs, including autism. ("I drink a whole pot of coffee with this group," he grins.) He is known fondly for his "Lo-Chow" routine, an affected dialect he strategically interjects when he notices that student attention is waning. He weaves among the desks, often giving a student a little squeeze on the shoulder. His feedback is constructive: "What was it like for Johnny in the first part of the book? Is he picked on? Does he beat up people?" or "You've covered this part . . . which I like. . . . Now you need to include . . ." If he sees a common misunderstanding as he monitors, he'll say, "Everybody freeze" or "All eyeballs on me," and reexplain or clarify the problem for the entire class.

Mr. Fox admits that teaching the students in the academically and intellectually gifted (AIG) block gives him a needed change of pace in the latter part of the day. "They're considerably more cerebral," he grins. He frequently collaborates with another AIG teacher for literature discussions and special projects. During one unit, the students studied real speeches delivered during the early stages of World War II, which were related to the political and ethical use of atomic weapons. Included were those of Harry S. Truman and Robert J. Oppenheimer. As a culmination, "The Drop Decision" debate between the two classes was scheduled in the school media center. Teams of students assumed the role of opposing advisers to President Truman, played by an outsider, before the United States dropped the first atomic bombs on Hiroshima and Nagasaki.

The presentations/debates took place over a three-day period, and parents and other classes attended. Student teams were responsible for preparing and presenting a five-minute persuasive argument. Two minutes were allotted for question-and-answer, and thirty-five minutes for debate and closing arguments. The youngsters were also in charge of the media center layout and any visual enhancements.

As with the heterogeneous classes, Mr. Fox's methodical planning is evident. He consistently aligns curriculum standards, instruction, and assessment, and he concentrates on the individual progress of these more advanced learners. The debate project, for example, incorporated research and persuasive writing competencies in addition to the refinement and application of grammar skills. In his biweekly newsletter to AIG parents, he is explicit about his intentional focus on student learning progress. An excerpt from the *AIG Agenda,* published to keep parents abreast of daily work, special projects, and instructional policies, follows:

Our Grammar Policy . . .

We believe that there is nothing worse than teaching grammar in isolation. Knowing this, we are working to incorporate focused areas of grammar into every writing and presentation that the students create.

Until now, we have worked on building a grammar base to ensure that our students will understand the terminology we use. Our first application will occur with the presentations used in the debate.

Our focus will be on using consistent verb tense. We are pleased with the progress of our students thus far. They have spent many hours building solid grammar fundamentals so that they may apply them to real-world situations.

Mr. Fox describes his personal classroom management style as varied: It changes according to the needs of his students. "Some of my classes are highly structured and some are free-flowing," he notes. "I try to manage a class more through personality and relationship principles than a fixed set of rules." His teaching philosophy is tied closely to his views about young adolescent development. He speaks of the cyclical nature of their moods and levels of maturity, and stresses the need for balance of freedom and limitation. He might let students sit where they choose at certain times, but if they demonstrate an unwillingness to learn there, the arrangement is made *for* them. He applies this view to their learning as well: "They can gain some autonomy and ownership over their learning, but I will curtail that privilege when the need arises. I try to treat them as individuals. I do *not* believe that fairness means treating every student the same way."

Mr. Fox's high expectations are evident in other ways. When no one wanted to walk along the ramp to the lunchroom with an autistic student, he addressed the situation directly with zero tolerance for disrespect. During a discussion, when a student laughs at another's response, he simply says, "Ignore her. I'm focused on you." When two students pass a note, he says, "Excuse me," and reaches behind him to intercept the piece of paper. When two others begin talking, he turns and indicates, "You're making me forget my argument." Shirts are to remain tucked in. He also gives very little homework except for test preparation. "We work from 'bell to bell.' They have a life outside of here."

With a BA in English education, Mr. Fox has taught every grade in his 6–12 licensure span. For two of his eight years of experience, he was an assistant principal and athletic director at a middle school in the eastern part of the state. His coaching record includes head girls' varsity track and head boys' and girls' varsity basketball at the high school level. In his current position at Turrentine Middle, he is head football and basketball coach. Mr. Fox admits that he might be a bit more "gruff" with the four football players in second block. Nevertheless, when asked what he thinks about Coach Fox as a teacher, one of these athletes responds, "He's nice. He changes voices. He talks to us privately. He breaks it down so that we can understand. He really cares about us."

QUESTIONS FOR CONSIDERATION AND RESPONSE

1. In what ways does Ms. Dennison manage by high engagement?	
Ms. Dennison's management by high engagement consists of <u>fast-paced instruction, maximal use of time,</u> and an <u>intellectually compelling content</u>. Her <u>game show</u> approach during the test review catches the young adolescents' attention immediately. She also <u>varies their tasks</u> from individual to shared to collaborative, alerting students to the changing directions prior to <u>transitions.</u> She sets <u>high expectations</u> that students understand and use scientific terminology and concepts, and she helps their learning through storylike explanations and <u>humor.</u> She lets them <u>talk and move.</u> Ms. Dennison also <u>elicits a high level of thinking</u> (clarification and elaboration of responses, analysis, and synthesis of ideas) through her questioning and follow-up probes. She uses a <u>variety of teaching strategies</u> (demonstration, board notes, discussion, cooperative learning groups), and she <u>continually checks for student understanding</u> through questioning, visual monitoring, task response, and informal pre- and postassessment (clarify your mush!). Ms. Dennison also engages students through <u>choice</u> in projects and assessments methods.	*Reader's Response:* How can I use these ideas in my own teaching?

(Continued)

(Continued)

2. How does Ms. Dennison create a positive environment for learning? How does this impact classroom management?	
The positive nature of Ms. Dennison's classroom environment is reflected in the <u>humorous yet expectant</u> way she interacts with the students, which conveys the message that she likes them and values their thinking. She also <u>moves among the students,</u> putting herself physically and energetically into her teaching. The surroundings in her room are attractive and simple. She wants her students to succeed, or to <u>"let their smart out."</u> The seventh graders <u>know where Ms. Dennison stands</u> on issues such as grooming and dress. She relates to their developmental changes and challenges, and she believes that they will try to make healthy personal decisions when given choices. She makes herself available as a <u>facilitator of learning and as a human being.</u> The relationship Ms. Dennison has established with the students, in addition to the high expectations she sets for their learning and intellectual development, leaves little room for inappropriate behavior. <u>When actions have to be addressed, she does so firmly, without taking personal offense or holding a grudge.</u>	*Reader's Response:* How can I use these ideas in my own teaching?
3. Why did the young adolescents respond positively to the choice of unit assessment? How is giving choice a developmentally responsive strategy?	
Young adolescents feel important and personally regarded when they are allowed a voice in their learning experiences. Intellectually, <u>they are ready to think about their own learning (metacognition)</u> and how they might best demonstrate what they know. An opportunity for choice also fosters in young adolescents the belief that they can successfully direct their own learning (<u>self-efficacy</u>). Allowing options	*Reader's Response:* How can I use these ideas in my own teaching?

(Continued)

also encourages creativity, personal expression, and an appreciation of individual differences, each important in the <u>development of positive self-esteem and self-identity.</u>	
4. Why do you think looping has been a workable strategy at McDougle Middle?	
The sense of community in Ms. Dennison's classes is heightened by the continuity of a two-year looping experience. Interpersonal <u>relationships</u> are better established, and personal expectations for learning and self-management are affirmed. More meaningful <u>connections with families,</u> important to young adolescent schooling experiences, also form as a result of longer time for association.	*Reader's Response:* How can I use these ideas in my own teaching?
5. How would you compare the management styles of Ms. Dennison and Mr. Fox?	
Mr. Fox similarly manages through <u>high-paced instructional presentation</u> and a winning sense of <u>humor.</u> His interaction involves <u>physical proximity</u> in spite of the limited space in the mobile unit. Mr. Fox holds <u>firm expectations for academic mastery</u> and <u>respect for others' learning.</u> He motivates students through questioning, opportunity for <u>movement,</u> and a <u>variety</u> of instructional experiences that include whole-group discussion, cooperative tasks, technology, small-group minilessons, and student-led projects. Both Mr. Fox and Ms. Dennison manage on the premise that when young adolescents are meaningfully engaged in learning, there's little time to misbehave. Though both teachers use assessment (traditional, performance-based, informal) advantageously, Mr. Fox's forte is in the <u>individualized assessment</u> plan that enables him and his students to monitor learning progress on a daily basis. By systematically attempting to meet the diverse	*Reader's Response:* How can I use these ideas in my own teaching?

(Continued)

(Continued)

needs of his students through <u>differentiated learning tasks,</u> he minimizes frustration and maximizes achievement, particularly in the morning block. The focus is on learning and mastery with the expectation for behavior that supports it. The <u>assessment-driven management</u> system helps Mr. Fox to track progress and structure instructional tasks; it enables his eighth graders to assume <u>increasing responsibility</u> for personal learning and actions as they prepare for high school.	
6. What is the benefit of flexible grouping on young adolescent learning?	
<u>Flexible grouping</u> is a critical component of instructional practice that accommodates individual learning needs and interests. It is <u>progress based</u> and <u>achievement oriented,</u> enabling young adolescents to sense personal accomplishment. It thus <u>engenders competence</u> that positively affects students' attitude toward learning.	*Reader's Response:* How can I use these ideas in my own teaching?

3

Shifting Speed—
Not Lowering
Expectations

The three language arts teachers in this trilogy teach three blocks of young adolescents during the school day, each with uniquely differing learning needs. Within a four-minute time interval, the teachers transition from a class of homogeneously grouped advanced learners to an inclusion class where approximately 50 percent of the students have individualized education plans (IEPs). The personal management style of the three teachers differs notably, yet each maintains high expectations for academic learning and student self-management, regardless of academic level or special learning need. The key, according to them, is to find a way to reduce complexity without denying any student the opportunity to try.

Melaine Rickard, an eighth grade language arts teacher at Turrentine Middle School in the Alamance-Burlington Schools, approaches the challenge of student diversity with meticulous planning, calm demeanor, and clockwork pacing. She uses a range of instructional techniques, with well thought-out variation, and she communicates to all students her belief that each can succeed.

In neighboring Guilford County, Lisa Wilson believes that all students should have the opportunity to learn in a meaningful way, and she proceeds with undaunted determination. The Teacher of the Year at Eastern Guilford Middle, she embraces new instructional strategies and makes them available to all blocks, with strategic adjustment. If it doesn't work as well as she likes the first time, she simply tries again.

Michael Armstrong teaches eighth grade at Hawfields Middle School, another school in the Alamance-Burlington System. A twenty-year veteran, he operates on a similar premise: Interesting and challenging instruction motivates young adolescents to engage in learning. The more meaningful the learning, Mr. Armstrong firmly believes, the fewer the discipline problems.

A *SILENT SEMINAR??*

Case Study 3

The time is 12:20. Ms. Rickard stands by the overhead projector at the front of the classroom, her blue pen poised over a sheet of acetate labeled "The Ninny." The eighth grade language arts class returned from lunch at 12:05 and read the Chekhov (1991, pp. 159–60) short story silently. Their goal while reading the two-page classic was to think about its theme and about their personal reactions and responses to this central idea. While they read, Ms. Rickard had quietly circulated among the desks, having students choose a color of Magic Marker from a plastic bucket. "Raise your hand and share your reactions," she begins, and soon her neat handwriting fills the transparency with the students' responses:

> The guy is mean.
>
> ✓ The guy is deceitful.
>
> He plays tricks on the maid.
>
> ✓ The man is so controlling that she's frightened.
>
> Takes place long ago and not in the United States.
>
> I felt bad for the maid. She doesn't stand up for herself. She is shy.
>
> ✓ She's so poorly treated that she thinks it's normal.
>
> ✓ She thinks standing up for herself is disrespectful.
>
> ✓ Did they have rights back then?

"I'm going to narrow these down to five," Ms. Rickard continues, switching to a red pen to place the check marks. As she gives directions for the upcoming task, she transfers each checked selection with a Magic Marker on separate sheets of chart paper. "When I call rows, I want you to go around to the charts and respond in writing to three of the ideas. Put your initials by your comment. You can agree or disagree. You can respond to what someone else writes or you can raise new discussion."

Opportunity to Think Critically

"It's like a circle discussion but with *no talking.*" She tapes the large sheets in five locations around the perimeter of the room, instructing students to look around and decide on their three selections. "Test your markers," she directs. "Live up to my expectations. Don't say a word. You can begin when I start the

Figure 3.1 Silent Seminar

Purpose

To encourage all students to respond to text because it provides a "safe" unspoken method of encouraging dialogue among class members. Another advantage for young adolescents is the "game" of moving yet not communicating except on paper.

Method

1. Students read a selection or section of literature, silently or orally as a group.

2. Students are asked to share with the class reactions and responses, ask questions, or quote passages that grabbed their attention while the teacher records offerings on board or overhead.

3. Class votes on Top 10 (or another number), which are transcribed onto separate sheets of butcher's paper around the room.

4. Each student is given a marker and the "silent discussion" begins. They choose three of the posted ideas and respond in writing, followed by their initials. The game part is that no one can speak or interact except to each other's comments on the charts. Responses may be in the form of other questions, proposed answers, affirmations, and disagreements. Teacher modeling may be needed.

5. Play appropriate music during activity to reduce "noise of silence."

6. When allotted time ends, posters are removed and returned to the owner of the question or comment. This student then leads, with teacher support, a discussion of any further questions that arise from the sheet. Posters may be placed back on the wall for future reference or review as reading continues.

SOURCE: Used with permission from M. Rickard, Turrentine Middle School, Burlington, NC, in *Managing the Adolescent Classroom: Lessons From Outstanding Teachers,* by Glenda Beamon Crawford. (2004). Corwin Press, Thousand Oaks, CA. www.corwinpress.com.

music." As sounds of a techno version of a Beethoven classic fill the Turrentine Middle School classroom, the twenty-five students move quietly from their seats, separating randomly into small lines in front of the posted charts. Their markers are already uncapped. Thus Ms. Rickard's silent seminar begins (see Figure 3.1 for a description of the task).

With ten years of teaching language arts to adolescents, Ms. Rickard has been called by teammates the master of organization. Beside the lesson planner opened on her desk is a To Do list with a few neatly printed items. Teacher and student supplies are organized on shelves around the room, all clearly labeled. It's Ms. Rickard's first year teaching science in addition to language arts, which explains one shelf devoted entirely to science materials. Plastic buckets hold colored Magic Markers. A "Been Absent" folder is hung on the wall next to the door for students to check for handouts. On another folder, posted by the filing cabinet near her desk, is printed, "Notes for Substitute Teachers." The day's agenda for each of the three blocks she teaches is written on the whiteboard, accompanied by homework assignments and project due dates.

Along the top of the front and back walls of Ms. Rickard's room runs a wall-paper border of books. A fabric swag drapes up and down over the tops of two side windows. A mirror hangs at the back of the room on the wall beside her kitty-cornered desk. Taped to the side of the overhead projector in the front is a colorful strip of paper with the words "I love teaching." A decade of experience teaching adolescents has shaped Ms. Rickard's philosophy about managing a class of young adolescents. "Difficulties at home and with friends, time of day, month, or year, and hormonal changes all affect an adolescent's behavior," she assesses. "They are more peer oriented than any other group. We must harness this and use it in our instruction and management."

> They are more peer oriented than any other group. We must harness this and use it in our instruction and management.

Ms. Rickard's organizational prowess is further reflected in the way she manages instructional time. All classes begin with a warm-up that is projected on the overhead as students enter. If a student finishes early, Ms. Rickard has a book, magazine, newspaper, puzzle, or brain teaser ready to hand out. Her ability to manage tasks concurrently, such as when she wrote on chart paper while giving directions for the seminar, saves instructional minutes. All student tasks are prefaced with a time limit, and transitions, especially involving movement, run efficiently on her cue: "When I lower the music, you should begin moving back to your seats. When the music stops, you should be seated." Her cues about subsequent learning tasks also serve as a time-saver: "When we get back from lunch," she had told the eighth graders prior to the seminar, "we will read a story about a character and then have a new way of talking about it—a game—so talk a lot in the cafeteria!"

Ms. Rickard additionally capitalizes on every minute of instructional time available. In the brief interval before lunch and the afternoon silent seminar, she had quickly reviewed the literary element of the theme, comparing it to a moral or message. Students were asked to copy the definition, which was handwritten on an overhead transparency, into their notes. Her question, How do we figure out the theme? helped to remind the students there was an "easy way" (directly stated) and a "harder way" (making an inference) to determine the theme in a story. When they returned from lunch, the eighth graders anticipated what would happen and what might be expected of them. They were prepped and ready to progress into the next half of the lesson.

> Personal accountability for acceptable actions.

Ms. Rickard's expectations for student behavior focus on personal accountability for acceptable actions. She believes that "no matter what baggage you bring to school, you can be respectful," and she models this respect in the way she interacts with students, correcting firmly with a smile and a "Please." "Adolescents will respect you if you are strict and fair, not wishy-washy," she acknowledges. "Teachers can be *proactive* in many ways, but we still have to *react* to many situations," she continues, verifying that the manner in which the disciplining is communicated is important. Her classroom rules, posted above the whiteboard on the wall in front of the class, project her beliefs about young adolescents' ability to learn to manage their own actions:

Be responsible for your attitude.

Be responsible for your actions.

Be responsible for your work.

Respect yourself, others, and property.

Follow all school rules.

A small sign posted over the pencil sharpener additionally reinforces this daily message: "You are responsible for your actions."

Ms. Rickard's high expectations for student self-management are paralleled by the standards she sets for the young adolescents' academic achievement. A poster on the front of her door speaks to all blocks: "Welcome to class! You may start thinking now." She is firm in the declaration "I don't like the concept that this is too hard for my kids." With these high expectations, she does make some allowances when she grades. "I ask myself," she explains, "Is this the best this kid can do? My expectations are relevant to where they are." In a school where strong instructional practice is expected, she uses a variety of methods and grouping strategies to facilitate student learning. One approach is working well during the inclusion block an early morning in late October. The class, comprised of twenty-six eighth graders with a range of special learning needs, has an approximate 50:50 ratio of Caucasian and African American. On this day, the class is getting set up for a Jeopardy-style test review on Philbrick's (1993) popular young adolescent novel, *Freak the Mighty*.

> Teachers can be *proactive* in many ways, but we still have to *react* to many situations.

> My expectations are relevant to where they are.

It is 8:45 A.M. and Tacky Day at Turrentine Middle. Ms. Rickard is decked out in a chartreuse green polyester skirt and mismatched blouse outfit reminiscent of the 1970s. She can be heard numbering off students in a round-robin manner to form six teams for the game's competition. "Now listen," she directs. "When I call your number, I'll show you the area where I want you to move." The thirteen-year-olds move as directed and settle into new seats. After allowing them fifteen seconds to select an "answer person," Ms. Rickard continues with the rules for play. Like the broadcast game show, each team is expected to choose a category and item value ranging from 100 to 500.

On the whiteboard, Ms. Rickard has reconstructed the game's format, which she reveals when she pulls up the overhead projector screen. Categories include Literary Elements, Character, Plot, and Conflict. A fifth category is labeled Important Things. Point value is marked on colored sheets of construction paper taped to the board. The directions are simple: Students will select a category and item value and Ms. Rickard will pose a corresponding question. Any unrelated talking will lose a team 100 points, she indicates. To make a point, Ms. Rickard announces that if the real game had begun, Team 1 would already be down 100 points!

The game is launched with the first team's choice. For 300 points in the category of Character, the name "Loretta" is uncovered. Ms. Rickard's clear voice can be heard: "Who is she and why is she important?" As the first team discusses a response, she cautions the class to listen: "These are things you'll see on your test." The game continues as "Gram and Grim" are uncovered under the category of Conflict for 500 points. "Ten seconds. I need your response." Ms. Rickard is firm. When an incomplete answer is given, however, she probes, "There is another part to that. Think about the beginning of the story." After another few seconds, when the team can add no additional information, Ms. Rickard offers the question to another team. Hearing a correct response, she awards partial credit to both teams.

Play continues in a rapid interchange of selection, response, praise, and probing. Ms. Rickard, whose diminutive figure is obstructed from view at times by the sizable thirteen-year-olds, maintains apparent command. In a competitive spirit, the teams often choose the 500-point items as their first choice. Ms. Rickard records the scores on the whiteboard. Smiling a lot, she gives an occasional hint: "This person was a cretin. That's one of our vocabulary words." At one point, a team objects to a partial-point award. Ms. Rickard grins, waves them away with her hand, and the complaining stops.

A couple of times during the game, when the students' excitement gets the better of them, she offers a "Sh! Sh!" but points are not deducted. Once she needs to warn a male student about showing good sportsmanship. She reminds students to continue to listen: "These are test questions." As the allotted time nears an end, she calls for a final bonus question. Each team can wager up to 500 points, which all of them confidently opt. Green slips of paper with team numbers on the top are distributed for answers. "Remember, if you talk, all bets are off. You may whisper." She extends the culminating bonus question, "Who is the narrator?"

Ms. Rickard tallies the points, and the scores are quite close. She announces that their reward would be candy with the next day's test as she directs the students to return to their original seats. The last section of the block will be spent working with partners on their novel projects. She had given the choice: The students could construct a plot map of illustrations on the novel that included setting, main characters, plot line, and theme, or they could write another chapter of at least three pages to the novel. When the eighth graders are slow to make the transition, she turns off the light. In a stern voice, she cautions, "OK. We'll try this again. This last thirty minutes is for working on your projects. Now shift gears."

Firm Expectations for Personal Behavior Management

"You understand the guidelines. Work with your partner only. If we need to stop again for noise, this becomes individual."

Ms. Rickard switches the lights back on and the students settle. Two girls begin work at the single computer in the back of the room. Ms. Rickard scans the room and asks a couple of boys to come show her "what they've got." She suggests that one work on describing the main character and that the other write on the poster, and explains, "That way, each of you has a responsibility." She makes a similar recommendation to another team. To one student she directs, "Are you working on the main character? Give me some describing words." To a boy who is stalled on the plot diagram, she says to think about big steps in the story "as if you were to tell it to someone."

The class period closes and Ms. Rickard reminds the students that the format of the upcoming test will not be open book. "Use your brains!" She smiles and praises their cooperation during the review. As the students leave for a restroom and locker break, she quickly readies the board for the next block.

The time is exactly 10:05 A.M.

"SHE NEVER STOPS TEACHING"

Case Study 4

Lisa Wilson characterizes her classroom management style as "fun, firm, and risk-taking." With seven years' experience as a sixth grade teacher, she has taught all content areas: language arts, social studies, math, and science. Her K–6 licensure prepared her well. Currently a sixth grade language arts teacher at Eastern Guilford Middle School in Greensboro, North Carolina, Ms. Wilson manages three differing blocks of active eleven-year-olds. Her morning begins with a class of advanced learners (AL). Later in the morning, a special education teacher comes in to assist with the range of special learning needs of students in an inclusion class. The afternoon class is heterogeneously grouped. Ms. Wilson was nominated by her colleagues to represent the school in the 2003 Guilford County outstanding teacher competition, and one of the school administrators anticipates a win. According to the Eastern Guilford's media specialist, Lisa Wilson is a teacher who "never stops teaching."

Ms. Wilson's classroom is located at the end of a long corridor designated Sixth Grade Hall. It is colorful, artistically decorated, and student-friendly. Even in late September, the look of the season is apparent. Paper black cats, pumpkins, and autumn leaves augment the room's entrance and front bulletin board. On the whiteboard at the front, Ms. Wilson has used alternating colors of brown and orange to distinguish each block's assignments, objectives, and homework. A large yellow and orange paper sun, sporting a pair of sunglasses, is suspended from the ceiling. A long row of windows along the side of the room opens to a view of green lawn bordered with trees. In the back corner sits a large blue beanbag chair, a popular spot for student reading and small-group work.

A stapler and three-hole paper punch are available on a small front table near the board. Other supplies, including tape, glue, and scissors, are located in the student materials cabinet. Asked about the physical layout of the classroom, Ms. Wilson notes, "Everything has a place. Students know that and are expected to put things away." On a "Keep Informed" bulletin board she posts a grading scale and a large laminated calendar. Written on the acetate squares are project due dates, school events, and other reminders. Popsicle sticks on a large yellow star-shaped poster designate Ms. Wilson's classroom helpers. Under a "Happy Birthday" banner across the back wall are smaller stars bearing students' names. Once a month the birthdays are celebrated with brownies. The words "I can't" are printed in a circle that is crossed by a diagonal black line.

> Ms. Wilson manages the family-like environment of her classroom with definitive organization.

Ms. Wilson manages the family-like environment of her classroom with definitive organization. "I am borderline obsessive about being organized," she admits. "This helps me a lot in class. I don't spend time scrambling around looking for things I need. I think it also helps my students stay more organized." She secures her planner, similar to one given to all students by the school PTA, on a clipboard that she carries around during class. At the beginning of each period, she checks for empty seats, makes a note of who's absent, and gives a While You Were Out sheet to the class scribe to complete. Kept in Ms. Wilson's personal planner is also documentation of any student misbehavior that might warrant a reduced conduct grade. She additionally uses the planner to write down daily homework assignments in order to avoid any confusion when students are absent.

Ms. Wilson is similarly organized with her instructional planning. In fact, she admits that she *loves* to plan. With books and resources spread out around her, she maps out lessons that build on and connect to one another in an effort to reinforce learning for her sixth graders. She organizes instructional units in three-ring binders with an outline in the front. "It makes it very easy to pull items to copy or use in class and then replace in order," she explains. She also laminates overhead transparencies for easy washing and no marker stains. As soon as she teaches a lesson, she makes notes of what went well or where revisions are needed. She keeps the instructional binders year to year, changing, adding, and adapting as new groups of young adolescents come her way.

> With middle schoolers, surprise sometimes breeds misbehavior.

Ms. Wilson's daily ritual of prompt class start, warm-up activity, homework check, and planner check-off remains similar and predictably consistent. Essential questions ("big idea" content questions) and class plans are written in a designated place on the whiteboard. "With middle schoolers, surprise sometimes breeds misbehavior," she attests. The learning experiences within the overall structure of her planning, however, vary greatly. A self-proclaimed risk taker, Ms. Wilson is not hesitant to give a strategy a try—even a new one—and with any group of students. She realizes that many of her students do not get a great deal of reinforcement at home related to the love of learning. Many do not have computer access, and most need a little extra motivation.

Ms. Wilson's approach in teaching the wide range of learners in her classes, however, is "*not* lower thinking . . . *not* 'dumbing down,' but *rather* less complexity and more help." These beliefs and her risk-taking nature are evident on a morning in early November. Just the week before, Ms. Wilson had attended a workshop on reading in the content areas. Today she planned for all of the sixth graders to experience a "jigsaw" structure—with some of her own built-in variation.

Only a few minutes are left in Block I. The homogeneously grouped advanced students are still circled up in expert groups discussing the characters, plots, and vocabulary in one of three young adolescent novels. These include Paterson's (1977) *Bridge to Terabithia,* Babbitt's (1975) *Tuck Everlasting,* and Sachar's (1998) *Holes.* Originally, the students had indicated their first, second, and third choices, and most had been assigned to the expert group of their first choice. Ms. Wilson is roving around the classroom. The *Bridge* group is told to "Settle down, please." As the time ends and sixth graders prepare to transition to the next-door mathematics class, she reminds them about the substitute teacher. "Remember, he's a guest in our building. Act like Ms. Newman is still here, not like you're in a zoo." Her smile is serious.

> *Not* lower thinking . . . *not* "dumbing down," but *rather* less complexity and more help.

The second block might have benefited more from Ms. Wilson's reminder. They entered noisily, causing her to address them in a firm voice: "Students, you always have a warm-up. Settle down. Have your bottoms in your seat. The warm-up is on the screen." Less than a minute later, she adds, "Right now, all of you should be writing on Page 8 of your orange folder." For the starter, the sixth graders are asked to respond to the writing prompt, What do you like best in Part 1 of *Holes?* Each student writes in a response journal made of numbered pages of notebook paper and construction paper. Clipboard in hand, Ms. Wilson takes attendance. The exceptional children's (EC) teacher helps to monitor as the students write. "Three more minutes to finish," Ms. Wilson indicates as she places a copy of the Sachar book on each desk.

Sitting on a counter at the back side of the room is an old brown leather suitcase. Visible inside its opened lid is an assortment of objects: a shovel, a jar of jam, a water bottle, a large onion, a tube of lipstick, and one dirty tennis shoe. Each of these objects will play a role in the unraveling mystery at Camp Green Lake, the site of the juvenile correction facility in *Holes.* The protagonist, young Stanley Yelnats, has been sent there for an eighteen-month term. Ms. Wilson began the study of the novel with this hook: As each object is revealed during the class readings, each student is to make a prediction about its role in the unfolding story. Eighteen of the twenty-five students in this Block II have an individualized education plan (IEP). Ms. Wilson had a similar situation the previous year but without any in-room assistance.

On this day, with the reading of the novel's Part 1 completed, Ms. Wilson has planned for a cooperative learning task during which the students will analyze the main character, Stanley. She distributes a Character Analysis Grid (see Figure 3.2) and projects a transparency copy of the grid on the overhead screen in front of the class. She informs the students that they are going to become experts on answers to one of the four questions on the grid. They would then teach their home base group what they've learned. The numbered question highlighted in yellow on the handout grid is the one each student is assigned. These character analysis questions, which they will apply to Stanley, are also written on the front whiteboard. "Remember last week when we talked about conflict?" Ms. Wilson reviews. "What is Stanley's conflict?" One student, who

Figure 3.2 Character Analysis Grid

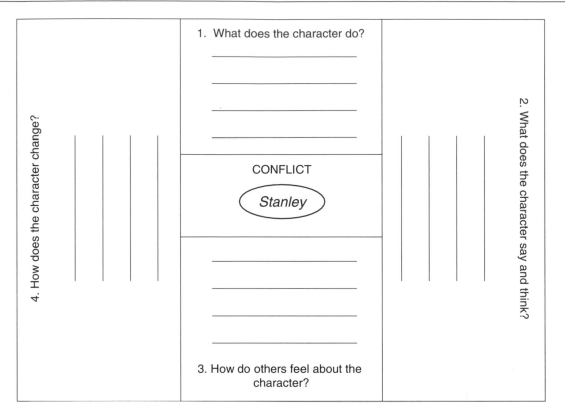

What do you think is going to happen to Stanley as we move into the second part of the story?

SOURCE: Character Analysis Grid from Buehl, D. (2001). *Classroom Strategies for Interactive Learning* (2nd ed., p. 153). Reprinted with permission of Doug Buehl and the International Reading Association.

had to be reminded to raise his hand, responds, "Stanley versus self." Ms. Wilson probes, "What is Stanley's problem with himself?" She reminds them of their previous discussion about Stanley's struggle with the idea of being accepted and how some adolescents always picked on him.

Ms. Wilson begins a countdown from 5 to 1 for students to move from original home base seats to their new expert groups for the activity. "When I get to 1," she informs, "everybody should be in a seat working with your assigned question group." Four groups of roughly five or six students are formed, and Ms. Wilson and the EC teacher circulate among them. "What does he actually do?" Ms. Wilson asks, to which a student in Question 1 group responds, "Goes to court." "Then write that down," she returns. One boy with peroxide-spiked hair, who had ended up in a group with four females, stands up with a loud burst, "I'm working alone! I've read this book five times and no one will listen to me." Ms. Wilson directs him to go out into the hall with her for a minute.

Addressing Unacceptable Behavior Promptly and Privately

When they return, he settles back with his group. Ms. Wilson addresses the girls, "Are we all being open-minded to everybody? Expert groups. That means we work together as a group."

A cue of "four more minutes to finish" is changed to "two," as some of the students appear restless. Ms. Wilson instructs that they will now restructure their groups, and asks them to move back to their original seats, "Please." "Five-four-three-two-one." She waits beside the overhead projector. "When I have everyone's attention, . . ." she says, looking around the room. "I'm going to wait because I'm pretty sure I don't have everyone's." She continues with directions for the second part of the task. With the students back in the original home base grouping, each student will take turns teaching the other three what he or she knows about the assigned question's response. She instructs them to begin with the first question and continue to the fourth in order. "So when you get finished," Ms. Wilson explains, "you'll have all your lines filled and all four questions answered." She points to the lines on the projected grid on the overhead screen as reference.

The second part of the cooperative learning activity seems to be working. Ms. Wilson cues the students that they should be finished with Question 1. "Expert 2 should be talking. I'd like for you to be finished with all four questions in the next six minutes," she informs. She looks around and asks one group why they weren't talking, just copying from one member's paper. "You should be teaching," she reiterates. With a stern look and a shake of her head, Ms. Wilson stops the spike-haired boy from trying to get the attention of a buddy in another group.

She explains the benefit of the activity.

A few minutes later, Ms. Wilson calls time, turns the overhead back on, and designates a student from Question 1 expert group to come up and write one response on the acetate. She continues similarly for each of the four questions. As the designated students are writing with the overhead pen, Ms. Wilson asks for "all eyes in this direction." She explains the benefit of the activity: "Hopefully it wasn't as intimidating as if you had to do it all by yourself. I hope you'll be able to chunk the information and to learn it."

As the rotation continues at the overhead, Ms. Wilson is visibly concerned with the lack of attentiveness from the rest of the students in the class. She began asking the sixth graders in the audience to tell her, in round-robin fashion, one thing they learned that they hadn't thought of before and not to repeat anyone else's answer. When this strategy does not focus the students' attention as she wishes, Ms. Wilson makes the call, "This is enough. I want you to put your seats back quickly. I am not finished with class, but I am stopping this activity because I am not pleased with your actions. I don't know if it's Monday or trying something new, but this is not what this class is about and you know that!"

Knowing When to Make the Call

Ms. Wilson explains to the group that the character chart is supposed to help them understand Stanley in Part 1. "As we move into Part 2," she continues, "we'll see a big change in Stanley and we'll try this again." She instructs the sixth graders to answer the question at the bottom of the Character Analysis Grid: "What do you think is going to happen to Stanley as we move into the second part of the story?" "I want to see all pencils moving," she emphasizes. The students are directed to put the page in their orange folders when they are finished with the prediction and then to get out their planners. They are given a quiz time handout for homework to help prepare for the upcoming test on the first part of the novel. As individual planners receive Ms. Wilson's initials of approval, she gives sixth graders the OK to visit lockers and prepare for lunch.

Since this Block II inclusion group will join the substitute next door after lunch, Ms. Wilson offers a similar warning, adding, "Hopefully, you've gotten all of your sillies out." She reminds them that the walk to lunch will be a quiet one. Lining the students up by groups, she praises their current behavior: "This is the best movement you've had in this class period. Can we walk to lunch this way?" Hearing a collective "Yes," she directs the students to stop at the end of Sixth Grade Hall and wait for her.

> If something doesn't work, put it away and try again later. Usually the second time it goes better.

Ms. Wilson believes that managing a group of young adolescents is different from working with younger or older students. "I try to give the freedom they desire and to teach responsibility for one's own self," she expresses. She adds that giving the students choices works well most of the time but that giving them too many "can make a mess." She advises that teachers should try a lot of new things all the time. "Keeps them guessing," she grins. She is quick to add, however, that it's probably better not to try something new and difficult on Monday mornings or Friday afternoons. "Brains are not fully functioning then!" She speaks from experience. She further advises with undaunted spirit, "If something doesn't work, put it away and try again later. Usually the second time it goes better."

"I TRY NOT TO FIGHT EVERY BATTLE"

Case Study 5

In his nearly twenty years of teaching adolescents language arts and writing, Mr. Armstrong has never faced a challenge equal to this year's—and to think he had requested it! Ten of the twenty-one students in his eighth grade inclusion class are identified with special learning needs, another by Section 501 of the Individuals With Disabilities Act (IDEA), and several have been diagnosed with attention deficit disorders (ADDs). Ms. Olsen, the EC teacher, and Mr. Armstrong have decided to team-teach Hawfields Middle School's first inclusion block—and they are determined to make it work. As the morning instruction begins on this day in early October, the tag team of teachers is ready for action. The thirteen-year-olds of Blue Block enter.

After a few minutes of sharpening pencils and getting settled, the students turn their attention to the whiteboard, where proofreading warm-ups are projected. This ritual of correcting a series of grammatical errors in two statements is a daily one. A chart of proofreading symbols is visible above the board for the eighth graders to reference. Before individual seatwork is finished, Mr. Armstrong elicits a volunteer to go to the whiteboard to begin making corrections in the first sentence. "OK, Tony. You're up, bud!" While Tony marks with dry marker on the board, Mr. Armstrong cues another, "Start moving that way. Tony's about finished. Remember, on Friday I'll pick three warm-ups to check. This is an easy grade. Don't let it slip!" Mr. Armstrong reminds.

During the warm-up, both teachers appear to be in continual motion: to the back, to the side, crossing over and behind, looking over shoulders and across at students' faces. All students have

In continual motion . . .

three-ring notebooks opened flat on their desks, and they are expected to make the necessary corrections to their work. "I see a couple of people with fog around their heads. Let's focus," Mr. Armstrong calls. He interjects explanations as the students in front continue to edit the projected sentences.

The layout of Mr. Armstrong's room is simple. Desks are arranged in rows, four long ones facing the whiteboard, five shorter ones turned diagonally on each side. In addition to the chart of proofreading symbols, a couple of motivational posters have been hung. Three colored journal boxes, one for each block, are situated on a counter near the side windows. Cubbies running along the interior wall are labeled with students' names. In the back right corner stands a carousel of worn paperbacks. Other books lean against the back wall on the counter below a cabinet neatly labeled "For Teachers Only." Ms. Olsen's materials are stored here. Mr. Armstrong's desk is located in the front to the left. The surface is not visible under stacks of papers and memos, and a large unopened shipping box of books sits in its center. Family pictures peer from a wall shelf behind, and leaning against one side of the desk is Mr. Armstrong's guitar.

The primary visual in the classroom is a 4' × 4' plywood board hung high on the wall above the row of cubbies. A student project saved by Mr. Armstrong from previous years in another middle school, this board is a large-scale and vividly colored painting of book covers with thematic representations of multiple young adolescent novels. Selections, among others, include *Where the Red Fern Grows* (Rawls, 1961), *Bridge to Terabithia* (Paterson, 1977), *Freak the Mighty* (Philbrick, 1993), *Tuck Everlasting* (Babbitt, 1975), *The Outsiders* (Hinton, 1967), and *The Giver* (Lowery, 1993).

On this day in September, Mr. Armstrong is beginning a study of another favorite adolescent novel, *Flowers for Algernon* (Keyes, 1959). He takes a quick hand survey to see who has read it. "I'm not feeling people are paying attention," he cues, and then asks, "What is intelligence? How are we smart?" Mr. Armstrong's approach to the novel is through the medium of Howard Gardner's (1993) theory of multiple intelligence (MI). The students are expected to rate themselves using a Likert scale, with Number 1 being "Not at all like me," and Number 5, "Definitely me." For Interpersonal, for example, the indicators include behaviors such as "I like being with people more than being alone," "I learn best through cooperative activities," and "I am good at communicating, organizing, and sometimes manipulating people."

Mr. Armstrong explains the exercise: "This is individual today, not committee. Shoot right from the gut. Don't worry too much over your answers." A girl holding a large stuffed green frog asks what Number 3 means on the Likert scale. "Danielle just asked a good question. Three means sometimes off and sometimes on," clarifies Mr. Armstrong. As he explains Gardner's theory to the eighth graders, Mr. Armstrong intersperses personal references. "I am an example of verbal-linguistic. I love to read and write," he offers, prompting a round of moans from the thirteen-year-olds. "My teammate, on the other hand, is interpersonal and logical-mathematical. She keeps me organized and is nice to you," he continues. "I heard Michael Jordan say in an interview one time that he sees himself moving in his mind before he shoots a basket. What intelligence would that be?"

The students are given time to assess themselves using the indicators and scale. As they are finishing, Mr. Armstrong uses a quick stand-up survey for each intelligence and allows students to share why they thought their preferences fit who they are. One female student, her arm adorned with a leather-studded bracelet and her hair streaked with orange, appears particularly delighted that interpersonal and musical-rhythmic are her strengths. The introductory self-assessment next moves into another task: The students are to design a picture that represents their intelligences. Newsprint and markers are distributed randomly. "Is this a project where you'll need other people?" jokes Mr. Armstrong. "No, it's an intrapersonal project. Be creative."

The eighth graders quickly spread out around the room. They work individually but talk freely to nearby classmates. Mr. Armstrong justifies the open-ended nature of the task with, "If I give them too many directions, their particular intelligence wouldn't come through." Both teachers circulate, cueing behavior, "Stacey, please be courteous." Periodically Mr. Armstrong calls out "Production! production! production!" One boy asks to go to the bathroom, and Mr. Armstrong responds, "OK, but hurry." The student picks up the pass and exits. Mr. Armstrong kneels beside a new Hispanic student to help and calls across the row to another Hispanic student to help him with a translation. "Check out my Spanish," Mr. Armstrong grins. "You need to take it in the tenth grade," came the reply. As time in the period dwindles, he alerts the group, "We'll stop in about nine minutes. Take home what you don't finish. Let's really think about production. Tomorrow we'll get paints from the art class and do a Rorschach test."

Time Alerts

The students begin what Mr. Armstrong refers to jokingly as their "migration" back to their regular seats. Some delay and talking trigger his warning, "I'm going to have to raise my voice. Let's move now!" In the last couple of minutes, when they are situated, he reminds them that their Giver projects are due on Friday. They can count on one hour to put the final touches on their work following a ten-minute vocabulary quiz. He walks over to his desk and, with obvious delight, opens his box on his desk. "Look! Good books!" he calls out as the students leave for their next block.

It's refreshing because these kids can sometimes make connections the academically gifted can't.

"They're loveable," Mr. Armstrong comments wearily after the Blue Block students have cleared the room. "It's refreshing because these kids can sometimes make connections the academically gifted can't," he continues. "But it does get intense in here sometimes. I don't want an adversarial situation. They had a miserable year last year, so we decided to try something different." With the assistance of the EC teacher, the arrangement seems to be working. Although it is only a couple of months into the school year, Mr. Armstrong is clear on one strategy: "I try not to fight every battle."

Holding a BA in English education and master of education in middle grades, Mr. Armstrong believes that mutual respect and a relaxed atmosphere are key to his personal effectiveness as a classroom manager. He describes Hawfields Middle School, in its second year of operation, as a school with a high focus on good planning and engaging lessons. This tactic helps to "minimize off-task and acting-out behaviors," he explains. "If students are interested and challenged, they are likely to behave better." He feels that this school, located in the eastern part of the Alamance-Burlington Schools, is a good fit for his personal style.

> If students are interested and challenged, they are likely to behave better.

Through his experiences in Grades 6 through 8, Mr. Armstrong has taught numerous adolescents. According to him, these young students try on different roles and often seem to be different people from day to day. He tries to tailor assignments and class activities, such as the multiple intelligence survey above, to help his students developmentally with this self-exploration. He is also cognizant of the intellectual potential of his thirteen-year-olds: "Eighth grade is most importantly a time where emerging abstract reasoning helps students decide what kind of people they will grow into being." As one of his colleagues comments, "The activities Mike uses are more than just appropriate for a particular novel or unit; his activities are always relevant to the lives of his students."

> Eighth grade is most importantly a time where emerging abstract reasoning helps students decide what kind of people they will grow into being.

Mr. Armstrong's approach to dealing with behavioral problems is aligned with his goal to help young adolescents realize and begin to direct their personal potential. He gets to know the student behind the behavior or the problem that underlies the action. According to this middle level veteran, "You have to look at what is good about a situation." He meets with students individually to discuss concerns, learns about out-of-school interests, and spends considerable time talking with students in more casual settings such as the hallway, ball games, or other school functions. One of these events was the school evening book fair and barbeque when his bluegrass band entertained. He speculates that he does more for in-class success when he's not actually *in* the classroom. He hands a book to a female student passing by the room during locker break and asks her about one she's reading at home. "She's grounded—can't leave the house," he explains. "I pass along a book to her every two

> It's all about the relationship I try to build with kids.

days." He sums it up with, "It's all about the relationship I try to build with kids."

Mr. Armstrong describes his disciplinary approach as positive though not assertive, and he admits that it's the harder of the two styles. "It takes until November to get things clicking, and depending on the particular group of students, the month may be January." By February or March he feels that he can focus more on content instruction. He laments that there is too much anger in schools today—on both sides of the teacher's desk. "I want kids to come into my classroom and let out their breath," he reveals. He genuinely enjoys teaching and interacting with his young adolescents and loves their humor and honesty. He also knows he will usually be assigned the so-called problem kids, which he acknowledges as "a back-handed slap of flattery."

Mr. Armstrong's assessment of young adolescence is nevertheless realistic. "It's a turbulent time," he ventures, "and students will use poor judgment and make wrong decisions." This was the case in late October when two students in Blue Block were suspended for bringing drugs to campus. It didn't matter that the drugs came from a parent's medicine cabinet; the lesson was one to be learned and the consequence was nonnegotiable. Mr. Armstrong admits, "The greatest challenge is dealing with the unpredictability of the early adolescence nature, the mood swings, the emotional backlashes, and the bad-judgment mistakes." With many years of teaching young teens, he is not discouraged. "We as teachers just have to seek and maintain perspective," he maintains. "If we're respected, we can be a significant influence on these students' lives."

> The greatest challenge is dealing with the unpredictability of the early adolescence nature, the mood swings, the emotional backlashes, and the bad-judgment mistakes.

Mr. Armstrong's beliefs about behavioral management are also evident in his concern about rules. If there are too many and they are meaningless, they are a turnoff for adolescents, who developmentally have a strong sense of what is fair and reasonable. According to Mr. Armstrong, rules should be logical, clearly justified, and, of course, enforced—with no bickering. He spends considerable time in the fall with discussion and role play about the use of good judgment and common courtesy. It is during this time that the parameters are set. Walking down the hall to the lunchroom, for example, he expects "no more than double-wide and no talking." If a behavior impedes their progress, the class simply walks an additional lap, passing by the cafeteria and losing prime minutes.

> Rules should be logical, clearly justified, and, of course, enforced—with no bickering.

Mr. Armstrong acknowledges that he makes no idle threats: He just "does it." Nevertheless, he stays cued in to his students' needs. One day he took a restless class outside for fifteen minutes, telling them to "run like crazy people." He maintains that his eastern view of time (not linear but *quality* of time on task) works best, particularly with the inclusion block: "The kids were appreciative," he remembers, "and were more focused when they returned."

Mr. Armstrong believes he's successful in his classroom management because he shows his students common courtesy: "I depend on the student *not* taking advantage. It works with 95 percent." He encourages teachers to be "blatantly honest" about why feelings might be hurt, but says, "Never let kids see they've gotten the best of you." In these instances, he will stop and have a class meeting. "This is how I feel when you're talking," he might say, or "When only one-half of you do your homework, is it the nature of the assignment? Are you being lazy? Let's talk about how to fix it." He reminds himself that parents "send us the best they've got" and that every student is "somebody's kid." As one of his student's parents expressed, "He's real. He shows the students that he is one of them."

Popular with students current and former, Mr. Armstrong is well regarded by colleagues in the school and district. A two-time local school Teacher of the Year, he has also received this honor on the system level. He is sensitive, however, to a perception that his success as a teacher might be related to what he calls a "cult of personality." The notion that he is successful because he is "cool" doesn't resonate. Sure, he sometimes rides his bike to school and plays a guitar; sure, he easily talks the talk of teens; and sure, he frequently weaves in personal stories during instruction. The real key to his effectiveness is not charisma but the

> His seemingly natural flow of higher-level questions, not reserved for the gifted block, raise students' awareness of real-world ethical dilemmas.

connections he strives to make. He believes that adolescents need people who will stop and let them express themselves, and they need to know that their ideas are valued. He admits he resists an antiauthority perspective ("I was paddled a lot in school!); yet he simply cannot treat students any other way than with respect. That's just the way he is.

Hand in hand with Mr. Armstrong's interpersonal management skill is a solid knowledge of content and pedagogical strategy. He answer students' questions without hesitation, makes uncanny comparisons, and forms relationships between ideas in seconds. He rewords definitions, concepts, and ideas until the "Oh yeahs" begin. As one colleague observes, "Mike is more than a teacher of facts and ideas: He is a storyteller of life." His seemingly natural flow of higher-level questions, not reserved for the gifted block, raise students' awareness of real-world ethical dilemmas:

- Should Charley have been given the experimental operation to expand his mental ability? (*Flowers for Algernon,* Keyes, 1959)
- Is giving up one's personal freedom of choice and decision making an equal trade for the absence of pain or physical discomfort? (*The Giver,* Lowery, 1993)

Through Mr. Armstrong's years of experience, one assignment that has been the most popular for all levels of students is the I-Search project. Students select any area of interest, formulate questions about it, and conduct concentrated research. The topics might range from in-line skating, dolphins, and mental illness to the Delta blues, and for one month the students literally "live"

Figure 3.3 I-Search Assessment

I-Search Component	Above Standard	At Standard	Below Standard
Why I chose this topic			
Introduction includes thesis			
Body contains topic sentences			
Covers all points on outline			
Each idea is developed			
Ideas area connected			
Paragraphs are unified			
In-text citation is used appropriately			
Conclusion summarizes main point without being repetitious			
Sentences are free of fragments			
Sentences are free of run-ons			
Sentences are varied			
Sentences reflect own wording			
Mechanics spelling			
Punctuation			
Works cited page—alphabetized			
Format is correct			
Source Cards format			
Note Cards format			
Notes			

SOURCE: Used with permission from M. Armstrong, Hawfields Middle School, Mebane, NC, in *Managing the Adolescent Classroom: Lessons From Outstanding Teachers,* by Glenda Beamon Crawford. (2004). Corwin Press, Thousand Oaks, CA. www.corwinpress.com.

the inquiry. They trek down to the media center to access the Internet, view streaming videos, take notes, and write. From this research they compose a detailed formal paper (see Figure 3.3 for an assessment criteria). The project culminates with an oral presentation to others in the class.

> More time, more structure, more help to organize information, and more reminders to focus.

Mr. Armstrong admits that the eighth graders in Blue Block may need more time, more structure, more help to organize information, and more reminders to focus. Their topics may vary from tractors to dysphasia, but the task helps them to feel a sense of accomplishment. According to him, "They're all going in the same place. Some of my students may take the interstate to get there. For the EC kids, it's like hiking."

The quality of the I-Search papers is a continual source of amazement to Mr. Armstrong. One student in a previous school wrote a thirty-page paper on the evolution of African American spirituals into the blues. He demonstrated the transition by alternating line for line the original spiritual music and the corresponding blues pieces. When another student did an I-Search on Doc Watson, he and Mr. Armstrong realized a common interest. Now a senior in high school, this student and three former classmates play with Mr. Armstrong in the bluegrass band. "The project gives students a chance to explore something they are *really* interested in and to share it with other students in an original and creative way," explains Mr. Armstrong. He adds that he just has to "sit back and be amazed."

> The project gives students a chance to explore something they are *really* interested in and to share it with other students in an original and creative way.

QUESTIONS FOR CONSIDERATION AND RESPONSE

1. What are some of the strengths of Ms. Rickard's classroom management style? Why do you think she is a successful teacher?	
Similar to Ms. Dennison and Mr. Fox in Chapter 2, Ms. Rickard manages through <u>ardent organization</u> that enables fast-paced interaction and a high level of instructional time devoted to academic learning. She clearly knows where she's going with her lessons and she <u>keeps the students alerted and prepared for each step and transition.</u> Her calm demeanor conveys self-assurance and expectation as she manages instructional and procedural tasks simultaneously (writing questions and giving directions, monitoring and distributing markers).	*Reader's Response:* How can I use these ideas in my own teaching?

(Continued)

(Continued)

Ms. Rickard is not hesitant to show a personal side through her laughter and participation in school rituals, but she <u>maintains a professional distance.</u> She is aware of the young adolescents' developmental needs for social interaction, movement, and playfulness, yet she sets high <u>standards for their content learning.</u> The use of the music for transitions is an effective procedural management strategy. Ms. Rickard also finds ways to help students reach these academic goals <u>(scaffolding) through motivating instructional formats</u> (game, silent seminar), <u>choice for projects, cueing, and feedback.</u>	

2. In what ways do Ms. Rickard and Ms. Wilson use the physical environment advantageously for classroom management? How is this use developmentally appropriate for young adolescents?

The physical environments in both teachers' classrooms have a homelike décor. Whether for sixth or eighth graders, the <u>settings are inviting,</u> colored and personalized with seasonal accents, wall-papered borders, swag curtains, birthday celebrations (more appropriate for the eleven-year-olds), and other visuals. Since young adolescents are very concerned about their appearance, Ms. Rickard's wall mirror is a strategic inclusion. The labeled and accessible supplies convey the two teachers' organization and give students a sense of security that materials are available for projects and other hands-on learning. <u>Order, security, predictability, and personalization</u> are classroom elements that meet the emotional needs of young adolescents as they seek to develop a healthy self-identity.	*Reader's Response:* How can I use these ideas in my own teaching?

3. How do the three teachers in this chapter create an appropriately challenging learning environment without compromising academic content in the inclusion block? What do you think is the relationship between engaging instruction and effective classroom management?

The theme of Chapter 3 is "appropriate challenge through meaningful and relevant instruction." Each teacher faces the reality of diverse student learning needs and <u>seeks a point of connection,</u> whether by ability	*Reader's Response:* How can I use these ideas in my own teaching?

(Continued)

level, readiness, behavior, or interest. As discussed later in Chapter 9, this approach (differentiation) <u>accommodates for diversity without compromising the quality of instruction or the opportunity to learn in a motivating way.</u> Ms. Wilson, for example, modifies a cooperative learning strategy by reducing its complexity. Students in the inclusion block focus on only one novel and are given much structure for movement and social interaction. They are expected, however, to engage in the higher-order thought processes for character analysis. Mr. Armstrong's I-Search task accommodates for differing interests, and he realistically anticipates extended time and help for research, organization, and composition. Ms. Rickard's game format for the test review is relevant and appealing to the students' competitive spirits, yet it is simultaneously rigorous in the literary content related to character, plot, and conflict.

When young adolescents' minds are engaged in motivating tasks that they can successfully complete, they are more compelled to put forth the needed effort and time. As successes accumulate, students begin to feel personally empowered (locus of control) to accomplish and ultimately to achieve by recognizing and using the appropriate resources and strategies (self-efficacy). The three middle level teachers diligently try to meet the students' learning needs and to <u>help them accrue positive academic experiences.</u> Though the process is exploratory and tentative at times, the benefit is reduced frustration and boredom, fewer related discipline problems, and a stronger commitment to learning.

4. How did Ms. Wilson deal with the inappropriate behavior of the inclusion block during the cooperative learning activity? How were her actions developmentally appropriate?

As noted in the Question 3 response, finding ways to appropriately motivate and challenge is not a definitive process, especially with the changing developmental needs and

Reader's Response: How can I use these ideas in my own teaching?

(Continued)

moods of young adolescents. As Ms. Wilson discovered by trial and error, even the day of the week can factor into students' receptiveness of a new instructional approach, which can consequently affect behavior. She <u>handled the situation with firmness</u> and an acknowledgment of these intervening variables, though she and the students would try the strategy again on another day. Young adolescents need to be able <u>to falter without harsh recrimination</u> and to have <u>opportunity to redeem themselves:</u> Ms. Wilson will provide it.	

5. In what ways might you compare Mr. Armstrong's classroom management style with the two female teachers? Consider the cognitive, affective, and physical dimensions. Why is he effective as a teacher and facilitator of learning?

Mr. Armstrong's comparable philosophy of "shifting speed" academically without sacrificing opportunity for relevant instruction and meaningful learning was addressed in Question 3 (cognitive dimension). He similarly tries to create an environment where adolescents feel valued and secure, although his approach is not evident in the physical trappings of the classroom (aside from family photos and books) or in his nonlinear view of time management. Mr. Armstrong's management strength lies in his undaunted ability over time, in class or hallway, within and beyond school hours, to make a <u>personal connection</u> with each of his students. This endeavor may take the shape of books passed along to a grounded student, a risk taken with rudimentary Spanish, or communication with a student's grandparent at a school function. Many of his students are at high risk emotionally and academically, and these connections are sometimes fragile. Those ties that do become firm, however, are powerful and lasting. The short-term benefit for Mr. Armstrong and his students is <u>a learning environment that is highly charged with the movement, social interaction, and authenticity of adolescent learning.</u>	*Reader's Response:* How can I use these ideas in my own teaching?

4

Shifting Responsibility to Students

A common theme in the two case studies in this chapter is each teacher's emphasis on student responsibility. Barry McDougald, the eighth grade language arts teacher in the Class Secretary case study, depends on students to manage class record keeping of absences and missed assignments. His time at Eastern Guilford Middle School can thus be spent more efficiently in getting the day's lessons started promptly. Besides, he believes the thirteen-year-olds do a better job keeping track of attendance, homework due, and handouts needed—and they love the "class secretary." On some days, Mr. McDougald's students play an incentive game called Star Wars. When students identify and correctly define any weekly vocabulary word embedded in the class reading, Mr. McDougald punches a small star on a yellow card. They can choose when to trade in accumulated stars for rewards.

The fifth graders in the Land of Woz case study at New Hope Elementary School are accountable in a different way. Each year it is John Waszak's students' responsibility to plan for and guide the younger students along the school's nature trail that circles the school property. They research information, prepare site lectures, and move classes of kindergarten through fourth graders from one station to another. At other times, teams of the ten-year-old "Wizards" take carts of the class critters, in glass cases and cages, to the lower grades where younger students are studying about animal groups and changes in nature. Wearing lab coats with official "Expert" badges, the Wizards give short talks about amphibians, reptiles, and mammals.

CLASS SECRETARY

Case Study 6

On the door of Mr. McDougald's eighth grade language arts classroom, in large vertical letters, is the word WELCOME. On the glass pane are taped several group pictures of students. Beside the door is another sign on which the message "Only positive attitudes allowed beyond this point" is written. Laughter can be heard as the door opens. Mr. McDougald is perched on a high stool at the front of the room animatedly sharing a personal story of his encounter with "Jaws," the paddle, as an elementary school student. In his hand is a copy of Roald Dahl's (1984) novel *Boy*.

The interaction is easy, a comfortable yet orderly exchange of questions and answers related to the story's setting. "I'll read a little more. Stop me when it's 9:38," Mr. McDougald instructs. At the specified time, he stops and asks students to get out their planners to record the homework assignment. Just before the thirteen-year-olds stand up to change blocks, one student goes to the front and shares a favorite quotation from the historical novel he's been reading. The class exits orderly and briskly. It's 9:41. Mr. McDougald turns on the music and begins greeting the next group of students with a big smile and cheerful "Hellos."

The colorful warmth inside Mr. McDougald's classroom at Eastern Guilford Middle School is a welcome contrast to the dreary fall day. A banner running the length of the whiteboard sends the message that "You are not finished when you lose. You are finished when you quit." A "Knowledge is power" mobile hangs from the ceiling. On a small poster is a quotation about attitude being a small thing that makes a big difference. A W.O.W. (Words of the Week) chart rises with vocabulary words on the side wall. A bulletin board with the title "Word-Up Wall" displays several students' weekly vocabulary word analyses (definition, phonetic spelling, and use in a sentence). Each paper is originally illustrated to reflect the word's meaning. Another bulletin board is trimmed in a newspaper border and labeled "Headlines." On a third, sporting an attractive fish background and titled "Explore Our Schools of Thought," are posted samples of the students' essays.

At the right side of the whiteboard behind Mr. McDougald's perch is a large multicolored poster with the words "Reach for the Stars." Underneath the title is a sequence of award levels for a competitive class game he calls Star Wars. Any correctly defined weekly vocabulary word, identified by a student during oral readings, merits a star. At the end of class as they exit, Mr. McDougald punches the students' cards with a small star image. The students also enjoy "stealing stars," which only happens when they can correct each other. Whenever students choose, the stars may be traded for a level of reward, numbered to reflect the cumulative value. The sequence follows:

1. A free pen or pencil

2. Candy or a late-work coupon

3. A raise-a-grade coupon

4. Hear your own music

5. A no-homework pass

6. Bathroom/locker break without penalty

7. A drop-the-lowest-grade coupon

8. Free computer time

Strategic Use of Incentives

Mr. McDougald's desk is positioned at an angle in the room's back right corner. On it lays a memo from the school parent organization for teacher teams to turn in nominations for a "Caring and Trustworthy" (CAT) student of the week on Friday. (The school's mascot is the wildcat.) Behind Mr. McDougald's desk on the wall shelves hang several personal pictures, most with students. A secondary English major, the gregarious Mr. McDougald was offered a teaching job at the middle school level in the Guilford County Schools, one of the larger systems in North Carolina. Five years later, he's still there because he *loves* teaching young adolescents.

Mr. McDougald admits that he needs help to keep ahead and "on top of" all that is expected of him daily in managing the classroom, so he has created several organization systems. His Calendar Box on the side counter consists of thirty-one hanging file folders, each labeled with a number that corresponds to the individual days of the month. On the front of the box is taped a paper monthly calendar. Each day Mr. McDougald places handouts in the appropriate file for absent students to check upon their arrival to class. Another box is labeled "Late Crate," for obvious reasons. Another of Mr. McDougald's prized creations is the Classroom Secretary, a blue three-ring binder located on a small table at the right side of the whiteboard.

"I found it hard to answer students' questions as they entered the room, to take roll, to deal with makeup assignments, *and* to get the class started, the part I really enjoy best," explains Mr. McDougald. Within what appears to be a simple notebook is an effective student-run system for classroom clerical management. Inside the sectioned binder are individual class rosters with dated columns. One student per period per month is selected to take attendance and keep notes of what is done in class. The next day,

> Within what appears to be a simple notebook is an effective student-run system for classroom clerical management.

or whenever the classmates return, it is the responsibility of the designated "secretary" to share with them what work they missed. To acknowledge that this communication is received, the absentees must sign the dated square.

On this particular day, a tall African American girl is in charge of the Classroom Secretary. As Mr. McDougald gets the students started on the warm-up, she takes the large notebook over to a male student, talks to him briefly, and secures his signature on the homework page. She returns the Class Secretary to the front table and takes her seat as Mr. McDougald says to the class, "By the time the music goes off, you should be finished with the opener." Three minutes later, he tosses a marker to a student volunteer to correct the grammatical errors in one of the sentences on the whiteboard.

The eighth graders are very attentive during the warm-up ritual as the student at the board marks the sentence with proofreading symbols. Mr. McDougald has announced that they will play Star Wars today and that a star will be awarded if someone sees an error made or one not corrected by the volunteer. "Be confident," he urges. "Something in your brain is telling you what's right." This encouragement is hardly needed, judging by the students' eagerly raised hands. Mr. McDougald probes about the proper usage of quotation marks around song titles and dialogue. He also kids the students about being too "picky" when they claim his period is not *visible enough* at the end of one sentence. Second on the day's agenda, which is written on the left side of the board, is Take 5, Mr. McDougald's name for journal writing. For the next five minutes, the eighth graders pore over the Take 5 sections of their notebooks, responding to Journal Entry #10.

The main lesson of the day focuses on the acquisition of five reading strategies: question, review, predict, connect, and evaluate. As with the previous block, the class has been reading the Dahl novel for literary context. Mr. McDougald holds up a sheet of notebook paper. He demonstrates as he instructs the students to fold it in half vertically and then into three sections. The goal is to make indentations for six equal-sized panels. Mr. McDougald calls the technique Listen. Sketch. Draft. He explains that the blocks on the left side of the paper would be used to name a specific reading. The corresponding (parallel) blocks in the right column would be used for sketching. "We'll visualize what happens in the story and transfer that image on paper," he indicates.

Before beginning to read the novel aloud, Mr. McDougald asks about its location. "What does capsize mean?" he inquires, holding up the cover of the novel as a reference point. He mentions a recent movie. With much voice definition, facial expression, and hand gesturing, Mr. McDougald reads aloud from his place on the stool. When he says the word *triumph*, he pauses and smiles. "A vocabulary word. Five seconds. What does it mean?" As it turns out, *triumph* is actually a vocabulary word from the previous week, but that is also fair game for Star Wars. "Good," Mr. McDougald praises. He again pauses when a new vocabulary word, *anesthesia*, is read. "Keep track of your stars," he reminds, and continues the reading, pausing periodically to ask questions or interject light talk. "Have you ever been away to camp?" or "Blood, ooh, I would have passed out . . ."

On the board behind Mr. McDougald's stool is a ten-block grid measuring at least two feet in diameter and four feet in height (see Figure 4.1). Inside each block is printed in capital letters one of the five reading strategies. Each word is repeated in a second column to give the students more tossing options and space from different seats and rows. After a few more passages, Mr. McDougald pauses with "Stop right now. Whom have I not talked to today?" He points, "You . . . you . . . you," and tosses a small sticky ball to a male student sitting two-thirds of the way back on the second row. The student, in turn, quickly tosses the ball toward the board grid, where it hits and adheres inside the block labeled "Review." Mr. McDougald instructs the class to write the word *review* in

Figure 4.1 Reading Strategies Grid

Question	Predict
Review	Connect
Evaluate	Question
Connect	Review
Predict	Evaluate

SOURCE: Used with permission from B. McDougald, Eastern Guilford Middle School, Greensboro, NC, in *Managing the Adolescent Classroom: Lessons From Outstanding Teachers,* by Glenda Beamon Crawford. (2004). Corwin Press, Thousand Oaks, CA. www.corwinpress.com.

the first block of the left column on their folded notebook paper. They are then told to write two sentences of review from a previously read section of the novel. The students then sketch a corresponding image in the adjacent block in the column on the right side of the paper. A few minutes pass. Mr. McDougald snaps his fingers and calls on three students to share an example of how they had used the review strategy.

The reading continues with Mr. McDougald's reminder to look for vocabulary words: "Remember, if I say the word, what?" A student responds, "Raise your hand and tell the definition." Before long, another star is awarded. When asked about the star system, Mr. McDougald laughs. "I found this incentive sheet that someone had thrown away of perforated three-by-five-inch cards that read, 'Congratulations on your excellent behavior. You are a STAR!'" He said that he asked himself, "How can I use this?" He felt that he needed some more incentives, but didn't want to keep up with anything complicated or costly. Walking down the arts and crafts aisle at a local chain store, he spotted a hole punch that made star impressions. The star card strategy was thus modified for his classes.

Though the game is not played every day, it is a favorite with the students. Mr. McDougald laughs that most of the eighth graders treat their star cards like a gold credit card: "I love it! It's the simple things that make the adolescents happy." He's seen the students accumulate fifteen to thirty stars in one quarter. Though they can cash them in at any time, some just want to see how many stars they can collect to compete with fellow classmates. Mr. McDougald indicates that he awards good behavior, academic success on quizzes and tests, good character demonstration, and triumphs in classroom games. "It's probably the best thing I've thought of since I began teaching," he attests. To emphasize accountability, if a student loses the star card, he or she must submit a composition on the topic of responsibility or wait until the next nine weeks for a new card.

Mr. McDougald concludes the day's reading in time to go over the homework. He asks the students to get out their planners, "Please," and record the assignment. He visually checks to be sure every student has one, asking a boy in the back, "Got yours?" The student holds up his planner. The overnight task is in two parts, and Mr. McDougald supplies a graphic organizer for each section (see Figure 4.2). First, the students are to define two new vocabulary words, use each in a sentence, specify the part of speech, and illustrate with a symbol. Second, Mr. McDougald asks the eighth graders to write four or five statements about how they could apply all of the five reading strategies to the historical novel each is reading outside of class. He reminds the students that all work should be put in the homework sections of their notebooks for him to check the next day.

Figure 4.2 Graphic Organizers for Homework

Word	In Syllables	Part of Speech	Definition	Symbol	Sentence

Book title: _____

Author: _____ Historical year: _____

Beginning page: _____ Ending page: _____

Question

Connect

Predict

Evaluate

SOURCE: Used with permission from B. McDougald, Eastern Guilford Middle School, Greensboro, NC, in *Managing the Adolescent Classroom: Lessons From Outstanding Teachers*, by Glenda Beamon Crawford. (2004). Corwin Press, Thousand Oaks, CA. www.corwinpress.com.

Time is given for the student Quote of the Day, and the students exit past Mr. McDougald for a bathroom break and their next class. One male student named Duran pauses to respond to a question about Mr. McDougald's class. "I don't write all that good, but he makes every-thing so interesting. I like the games along with the reading. It's my favorite."

Benevolent dictatorship—a guide on the side.

Mr. McDougald describes his personal class-room management in metaphorical terms: benev-olent dictatorship—a guide on the side. His short experience has taught him, however, that one technique may not be suitable for all students. Strategies need to also vary and include choices for students. What chal-lenges him the most is providing a sense of fairness: "That sense of fairness is mostly scrutinized when you, as a teacher, are doing what you feel is right and best for student learning." He admits that "dealing with the mercurial adolescent mind" keeps him on his toes. He tries to "mix it up" so that his management approaches meet the different learning and social needs of his eighth graders. On the first day of school, he greets the eighth graders at the door with a playing card. They file into the classroom to find a matching card taped on the seat of the desk. Once seated, the students write their names on a card taped on the desk table labeled with the various periods of the day.

Mr. McDougald also takes pride in having a "very student-centered" class-room. Tired of reminding students of his expectations throughout the year, he decided to type them for the eighth graders to keep in the front of their note-books. This Expectations Sheet delineates the class purpose, projects, reading incentives, late-work policies, grading scales, and rewards, among others. The students are supposed to read them, get their parents to sign them, and study them for their first test grade. Mr. McDougald shares that his goal is to "prepare these students not just for high school, but also for life." He is hopeful that the procedures he has set up in the classroom will make the students more accountable for their work and missing assignments, and in the way they treat each other.

Even though it's still early in the school year, Mr. McDougald's creative efforts to build positive class community are already paying off. Prior to parent open house, he had asked his students to create six-line bio-poems, which provided information about their families, friends, and personal inter-ests. He laminated the poems on colored paper. Returning these to the students, he asked that they cut their poems into a shape that reflected their individual personalities. He posted these shapes, which ranged from pizza slices, baseballs, and abstract concepts, around the room for parents to locate. He had also encouraged his students to come so they could show their work to their parents. At the end of the meeting, it was announced that his home base group had the best attendance for the night. The following Friday, with the $50 award, he bought pizzas, and the students ate lunch outside on picnic tables in full view of the lunchroom diners!

During another week, Mr. McDougald and his two teammates worked together to plan a team breakfast to introduce themselves to the eighth graders in the self-contained resource and English-as-a-second-language (ESL) classes.

Personal Outreach

Mr. McDougald's group was responsible for bread, pastries, and napkins. Reminders were posted on the team Web site and attached to progress reports, but the fear lingered that Friday would arrive with no food. To Mr. McDougald's delight, however, muffins, doughnuts, pastries, fruit trays, cookies, Pop Tarts, sausage balls, cakes, and apple pastries arrived in bountiful supply. The gathering was a great success and one that strengthened team camaraderie.

Mr. McDougald takes his work at Eastern Guilford Middle seriously. It's no wonder that a wooden plaque hangs in his classroom with the engraved words "Mr. Barry McDougald, Times-News Award of Excellence, 1999–2000."

THE LAND OF WOZ

Case Study 7

In spite of a soft, intermittent autumn drizzle, the Lindsey-Bell Nature Trail tours are proceeding as scheduled. In teams of three, the fifth graders have met at tables in the classroom to review site information and procedures. The Wizards now wait to be assigned a class of third or fourth graders and a starting time by Mr. Waszak. "I'm going to be the weatherman. If you hear my whistle in Morse code (two short for an *I* and one long, one short, for an *N*), the tours need to stop," he instructs. "Remember, if you have a third grade class, a teacher assistant will be with you. They're in charge of discipline. You're in charge of teaching."

Meaningful Involvement in Learning

On his cue, the first team walks to the head of a class of third graders lined up in the hallway corridor. Reaching the outside door of the building, two of the students lead the class down the paved walkway toward the trailhead; the third remains to hold the door until all the younger students have exited.

The role of nature trail leader for a Wizard in the Land of Woz is an earned one. First, the fifth graders must become experts about what the younger students will view at the various stations interspersed around New Hope Elementary School's spacious property. At the first station located outside the back entrance, for example, is the wildflower garden. Here bugs, bees, and butterflies visit a variety of flowers for nectar or pollen. What wildflowers can be identified? What distinguishes a fly from a bee? Certain insects visit certain plants. Why? What makes a flower especially attractive to a bee or to a hummingbird? What foraging activity can be seen, and does this activity result in efficient pollination?

Station 1 is only the first of twenty sites that include a pond, a rotting log, a miniforest trail, a rock outcrop, a power line habitat, and an evergreen community. At least twenty-five different kinds of trees, classified according to deciduous canopy, common understory, or evergreen, also grow along the trail in addition to numerous varieties of shrubs, vines, herbs, and ferns. Along the course, students might additionally encounter any of several identified species of birds, mammals, reptiles, and amphibians.

Being a nature trail leader, however, involves more than knowing each station's information: Selected Wizards must have a plan for engaging the younger students. According to Mr. Waszak, good trail leaders need to use good teaching skills to help their audiences relate to what they will be observing. It is evident that the three ten-year-olds, now stopped with their group at the wildflower garden, met Mr. Waszak's selection criteria. An excerpt from their minilectures at this station and two other locations follows.

Station 1: Wildflower Garden

This plant is called yellow jasmine. Bees are really attracted to it. Does anyone know why? Do any of you have a hummingbird feeder? Notice the special trumpet shape of this plant. The name for this leaf is a compound, like a compound sentence. Remember, more than one leaflet is called a compound.

Station 2: A Miniforest Trail (Near the Woz's Pond)

Does anyone know why this plant smells so bad? Its job is to attract flies instead of birds. These are wild blueberries. Don't eat them—just made for birds to eat. This is a wild cherry tree. Cherries are fruit and grow in trees. See this leaf. Every fruit tree has a jagged leaf.

The trail tour continues in similar interactive manner. One of the third graders points to a leaf on another tree and asks if it is a fruit tree because it has a jagged edge. At the Pine Woods station located in the woods at the school grounds' perimeter, the tour guides distinguish the pine tree from the hardwoods. Anyone know why the pine trees come up first? Because they can stand the heat. The young trees need the pine trees to protect them so they won't get scorched. The teacher assistant at times interjects to speak to excited third graders: "Let's be respectful. If you are not quiet, you cannot hear your guides." She asks one student to leave a spider alone because it has a job. At Station 5, the younger students sit on benches in the forest to learn about a rotting log. The Wizards identify the insects as termites that act as decomposers in breaking all the nutrients apart.

A clump of mistletoe, which is noted to be a parasite, brings a smile to one of the guides who informs, "Boys and girlfriends like to come here." The trail leaders continue to share their expertise. They liken the protective bark on the loblolly tree at Station 8, grown around the sapsucker bird's holes, to "scabs when you get cut." They supply details about an outcrop of volcanic rock at least 600 million years old and explain that at one point, the rocks were two to three times as old as dinosaurs. The younger students appear impressed.

As the group winds back toward the school to proceed to another station, Mr. Waszak is seen near the back door. He looks around at the tour groups now staggered on the trail and checks his watch. He directs one of the teams to go inside the building, where a volunteer beekeeper is giving a demonstration before continuing to another station.

Mr. Waszak and other environmentally concerned teachers at New Hope conceived the idea for the Lindsey-Bell Nature Trail in 1991 during the school's first year of operation. Enhanced by four Eagle Scout projects, the trail has evolved into its current status. Each Earth Day, a student-emceed, student-directed celebration is held throughout the school, complete with solar demonstrations, tree plantings, and salamander releases. On Earth Day in 1997, Mr. Waszak's fifth graders presented the school with a nature trail guide and dedicated the trail to two parents who were instrumental in helping to complete the project. Inside the student-designed yellow cover are rich descriptions about what can be viewed at each station, graphic illustrations, italicized vocabulary terms, and key questions.

Involving Parents and Community

A unique feature of the trail guide is the "clock-compass" locator system embedded in each text description. By directly facing the station post (the 12:00 position), for example, a visitor could easily check out a special tree at 5:00 five feet away. The text might read, "Note the stump-sprouted dogwood with a dozen stems (5:00–5') and the four-stemmed winged elm (12:00–10')." The trail guide also includes brief descriptions of each of New Hope's special trees, with their leaves illustrated, and lists of wildlife and other vegetation. On the back of the laminated cover are a scaled map of the station route and the following trail etiquette:

This is your nature trail:

Treat it with the respect it deserves.

Walk softly and be as quiet as a woodland animal.

Leave the living plants and animals in their home.

Do not pick or dig anything.

Stay on the trail (except when specifically instructed for a trail activity).

During his twelve years at New Hope Elementary in the Orange County Schools, Mr. Waszak has maintained high standards for students academically. He is similarly clear about his expectations for his fifth graders' personal behavioral management.

High Expectations for Personal Management

He gives the ten-year-olds a choice: They can be responsible or he will take charge, "and that's not as much fun," Mr. Waszak confirms. He believes that the students should be given the freedom to make good choices, and he expects them to act maturely. His class is reputed to be the most challenging at New Hope. The Land of Woz, according to "Mr. Woz," is not merely a preparation for middle school but for the responsibilities of life.

In addition to the role of nature trail leader, Mr. Waszak's fifth graders have other opportunities to develop personal responsibility. Posted on the back wall of the classroom is the Wizard Honor Roll. The ten-year-olds earn a spot there by demonstrating good self-management skills both in and out of his classroom. Mr. Waszak refers to it as the "responsibility honor roll." Selection for the honor roll doesn't begin until the second month of school, when the Wizards have had a chance to prove themselves responsible. There may be times when all of the students' names are on the list, but it is rare that all names remain all year. Some occurrence may bring a name off for a couple of days. For students who have trouble staying on for any length of time, however, Mr. Waszak takes a positive tactic: "You did a good job. What can we do to help you do this consistently?"

Frequently the fifth graders in the Land of Woz make the decision to remove their own names from the Wizard Honor Roll. A teacher from another class may have to quiet some unnecessary talking in the lunch line, for example, or the media specialist might need to correct a behavior in the school library. The Wizards know that they are accountable for personal actions, and they recognize when they have veered off course.

The students try hard to stay on the honor roll because showing responsibility in Mr. Waszak's room brings special adultlike privileges. An honor roll student is trusted to go into a fourth grade classroom during the younger students' elective time to use a computer during writer's workshop, for example. Wizard Honor Roll students also earn the privilege to walk unattended to the lunchroom, computer lab, bathroom, recess, electives, or media center. They do not have to line up with the rest of the class.

At the beginning of the school year, Mr. Waszak spends considerable time acclimating the fifth graders to his expectations for the Land of Woz.

Designated Time to Communicate Expectations

He introduces the Japanese word *kei,* which means the highest form of respect for self, others, and property. Through discussion of how *kei* might manifest in the classroom, they together set the expectation to respect the rights of all students to learn and achieve. Mr. Waszak and students also talk about the movie *The Wizard of Oz.* "I explain to them that I am as much a fraud as the movie wizard," he offers, "and that I cannot pour knowledge into their heads. They have to take that responsibility themselves. I can make the assignments more interesting, or include the fun stuff, but they have to do the work."

In line with the expectation for responsible behavior, Mr. Waszak does not address the Wizards as "girls" and "boys," but rather as "young ladies" and "young gentlemen." He explains that this choice is not an attempt to curtail their enjoyment as kids but to help them begin to believe that they can succeed through their own efforts. Middle school will bring its own set of challenges, and the students need to know they can make it, no matter the external situation or constraints. Nevertheless, he does realize that Wizards are ten-year-olds who need to move and talk and work and play together as they learn to take responsibility for their learning. During math he encourages them to talk to compare and explain the various ways they arrive at solutions. (He believes that if you can do it five ways, you know it!) During writer's workshop, the students brainstorm ideas and confer with each other over editing suggestions. They also talk about group presentations and minilectures.

> "Talking is not a bad thing in my classroom," Mr. Waszak indicates, but continues . . .

"Talking is not a bad thing in my classroom," Mr. Waszak indicates, but continues, "I may ask the questions, Are you discussing a problem or sharing your learning ideas? Are you being productive? Is the level of your conversation appropriate for the classroom situation?" A negative response to any of these can send students in the hallway to complete their conversation. They generally return more focused. Mr. Waszak might give students the choice to move away from each other because "together you're creating a problem." Wizards who have trouble staying on task might first receive Mr. Waszak's shake of head or a quiet sign, a wink, but if the problem continues, out to the hallway for two minutes to regain focus. On occasion Mr. Waszak joins the student in the hallway for a conversation about how he or she can show respect for other classmates who want to learn.

Mr. Waszak provides multiple opportunities during the year for the Wizards to take responsibility for both learning and self-management.

Multiple Opportunities to Assume Responsibility

Another experience the fifth graders eagerly anticipate is referred to as Critter Island. During a time when the students in the lower grades study animal groups or changes in nature, generally in the month of May, the Wizards schedule classes of twenty to thirty minutes for show-and-tell demonstrations. Donned in freshly ironed white lab coats, the Wizard expert teams welcome each class to the Land of Woz, which has been transformed into a vine-covered archipelago of papier maché volcanoes. Scattered among the volcanoes are the cages and glass terrariums that are home to an assortment of salamanders, frogs, snakes, and tadpoles, which otherwise reside on the counters around the perimeter of the classroom. Each Wizard wears a badge of authority: "Dr. Cates, Reptile Expert" or "Dr. Brown, Amphibian Expert." Mr. Waszak tries to schedule the sessions so that the Wizard teams can perform for the class of a previous teacher, a sibling, or a cousin. "It excites them to be able to show off what they know to someone they know," he explains.

> It excites them to be able to show off what they know to someone they know.

Critter Island is a culmination of the fifth graders' science/environmental studies. The different types of volcanoes (cinder cones, dormant, active, etc.) include one that opens up to show the insides. The ceiling of the room is draped with leaf-covered vines from which stuffed snakes and frogs dangle. Each of the visiting classes is led into the classroom by a Safari Leader, who is dressed in a vest and pith helmet. As the students step through the vine-covered door, they are met with a blast of moist air from a humidifier. The croaking of frogs can be heard from a hidden tape recorder, and outside the window is a waterfall. When the student guests are seated, the Safari Leader explains the volcanoes (part of their geology unit) and shows how magma forms inside. The Leader then introduces the animal group experts, who, holding a representative animal, share their knowledge. After the performance/demonstration, the visiting students are invited to hold or touch any or all of the critters. This routine continues in thirty-minute intervals throughout the day with a rotation of Safari Leaders and new expert teams.

Mr. Waszak explains that each expert must write his or her own script for the performance. If an expert stumbles or forgets important information, the Safari Leader is expected to assist with comments such as, "Dr. Brown, weren't you just telling me that all fish are cold-blooded?"

Accountability for Academic Learning

"Could you explain that idea to us?" In order to be a Safari Leader, a Wizard must earn expert status in all the areas related to the various animal groups. These Wizards have the responsibility to direct the performance and must improvise as necessary to keep the information accurate and the show moving. Mr. Waszak also points out that he is not in the classroom during any of the performances. He spends the time working on another project with students who are not involved in a particular performance.

At the request of teachers in the lower grades, the critters are also loaned out throughout the year. The Wizards continue to be responsible for the animals' daily care by visiting to feed and to tend to them. They also take the carts of critters to classrooms for briefer visits when teachers ask. During these occasions, the fifth graders conduct "expert talks" and question-and-answer sessions. They leave the carts of critters in a classroom for the remainder of the school day, if the teacher desires, to enable the younger students to study the animals more closely through center activities.

During July, a smaller version of Critter Island, minus the volcanoes, occurs when a few of the Wizards and Wizard alumni take the animals, and their personal expertise, to the annual three-day Eno River Festival in Durham. According to Mr. Waszak, their participation is a highlight for the Wizards, who receive many compliments on their knowledge and ability to answer questions about the critters and their care.

> Mr. Waszak tries to deliver assignments in varying and novel ways.

Mr. Waszak, a three-time recipient of district-level excellence in teaching awards, has taught at New Hope for twelve years. His licensure areas are many:

intermediate education (4–9), middle grades (6–9) science, mathematics, and social studies, and secondary (9–12) mathematics. He believes in getting students involved in their assignment. As evidenced from the nature trail and Critter Island, he attests that "students are more eager to learn if they know they will be teaching and sharing their expertise with others." He tries to deliver assignments in varying and novel ways, such as through the mail, printed on a newspaper advertisement, or in a Mission Impossible format. To further enhance the authenticity of their learning, he doesn't use the word *name* on a student's assignment or study sheet. Instead, he writes the real-world occupation of the person doing the work:

Biologist: _____ or

Mathematician: _____ or

Cartographer: _____ or

Wordsmith: _____ etc.

Mr. Waszak is aware that not all of the twenty-five Wizards assume leadership naturally, no matter how exciting the invitation might be. Personalities, academic levels, social skills, and degree of popularity vary among the young adolescents in the class. He takes a developmental approach to help the students build confidence and self-efficacy. He may teach shy or unpopular students something that the other students don't know, for example. The skill may be simple—how to shape an origami figure, plant seedlings in the garden, find the square root of a number, do animation graphics, or make a dream catcher. After learning the new talent, they teach it to a peer. Mr. Waszak believes that this approach helps with students' self-esteem, raises the level of respect from classmates, and promotes community in the classroom. It's a win-win situation!

> He takes a developmental approach to help the students build confidence and self-efficacy.

The physical environment of Mr. Waszak's classroom provides an appropriate backdrop for the dynamic and interactive learning experiences he crafts for the Wizards. Over the door at the hallway entrance hangs the sign "Land of Woz. Welcome."

Physical Environment as a Backdrop for Learning

His hand-painted nameplate on the door is decorated with a wizard in a purple robe with fur trim. The Wizards' book bags, in assorted colors and varieties, hang on pegs just inside the door. A cartoon adaptation depicts a classroom where a student's hand is raised; the caption reads, "Mr. Waszak. May I be excused? My brain is full." A large poster of Albert Einstein peers from across the room. The list of Rules for Learning includes respectful actions and language, appropriate dress, and responsible care for property.

On the counter space and cart space along the back and far side of the room are the critters' glassed and caged habitats. A snakeskin hangs from the ceiling in the corner. Suspended from the ceiling in other parts of the room are student book mobile projects (an alternative to the traditional book report format) and flags from various countries around the world. A bulletin board displays a full-size world map; another, the class letters addressed to His Majesty King George III. Each letter is illustrated and the edges burned to simulate antiquing. Occupying most of the remaining space along the perimeter are three computers, a low round table covered in supplies and materials in front of the whiteboard, several packed bookcases, and Mr. Waszak's desk.

Scattered randomly in the center of room are five hexagonal tables, each big enough to seat four or five Wizards and Mr. Waszak. In neat blue jeans topped by a colorful cotton shirt, sleeves generally rolled up, a multicolored tie, and reading glasses perched at the end of his nose, he is generally found seated at one of these. He might be conferring with students about their limericks during a writer's workshop or encouraging them to find another way to solve a math problem.

One additional area is unique in the Land of Woz: a small table area designated by a small sign as "Kansas." "If you go to Kansas," according to Mr. Waszak, "your learning is in black and white." This area is used as a time-out place for his students or other fifth graders in the school who might need it. It is definitely not a popular place to be, and no student chooses to remain long, certainly not one of the Wizards. After learning

> Only *you* can be in charge of your own learning.

with Mr. Woz, very few want to go back to Kansas. After all, this is the Land of Woz, where only *you* can be in charge of your own learning.

QUESTIONS FOR CONSIDERATION AND RESPONSE

1. What are the various ways that Mr. McDougald communicates that he cares about his students? What impact might this message have on their motivation to learn?	
Mr. McDougald has created an <u>inviting student-centered classroom</u> of color, display of student work, and artifacts from his own life. His <u>positive communication</u> with students and parents begins with school opening and extends throughout the year. He greets students at the door with smiles and he laughs often with them and at himself as he shares personal stories and reactions. He plans events that help the students feel important. Mr. McDougald's learning environment is also highly expectant academically, organized, interactive, and supportive.	*Reader's Response:* How can I use these ideas in my own teaching?

(Continued)

(Continued)

Participation is anticipated and rewarded, and <u>tasks are carefully structured</u> through clear communication and graphic organizers (board chart, homework vocabulary grids, literary response journals). <u>Students are held accountable</u> through questioning and ongoing work checks. The interrelatedness of these personal and academic elements contributes to the eighth graders' sense of well-being and their belief in their ability and motivation to learn.	
2. How are the Class Secretary and the star system advantageous to Mr. McDougald and to the personal and academic development of the eighth graders?	
Mr. McDougald uses the Class Secretary and star system as <u>responsibility builders.</u> Shifting some of the responsibility for administrative management to the young adolescents helps them to feel important to the class operation. It also enables Mr. McDougald to engage students academically more readily. Unlike many incentive schemes, the star system retains <u>an academic focus</u> and is used sparingly and strategically for vocabulary building and review. It also keeps the eighth graders engaged as they listen for <u>opportunities to show their knowledge</u> and to check that of classmates. Even with the responsibility to keep track of their own stars, the students don't cheat. The "game" seems to be more in the competition to show what they know than in the external reward of prizes or privileges. Developmentally, the star system is working to build <u>internal motivation</u> and <u>individual accountability,</u> important personal skills for the young adolescents as they prepare for the transition to high school.	*Reader's Response:* How can I use these ideas in my own teaching?
3. How does Mr. Waszak incorporate the element of fantasy and imagination into the reality of his classroom life? How is this strategy developmentally appropriate for the fifth graders?	
Young adolescents, particularly ten-year-olds, are captivated by fantasy and imagination.	*Reader's Response:* How can I use these ideas in my own teaching?

(Continued)

(Continued)

Stories of magic and the supernatural appeal to their youthful ability to suspend disbelief. Mr. Waszak, through the Land of Woz, has fashioned a world where modern-day Wizards can become champions of their own learning direction, if they so choose. Using the familiar metaphor of <u>finding power within one's own ability</u> from the more modern motion picture, he provides the fifth graders with numerous opportunities to develop responsibility and to demonstrate that they can take charge of their own learning and behavior. Through the imagery of wizardry, Mr. Waszak capitalizes on <u>students' natural interests</u> as he promotes <u>self-reliance</u> and personal accountability. Developmentally and in preparation for the expectations of sixth grade, this transition from <u>dependence to independence</u> is a critical step.	
4. In what ways does Mr. Waszak engender responsibility in his students? How do these management strategies meet students' social, cognitive, and personal needs?	
Mr. Waszak gives the Wizards numerous <u>opportunities to develop responsibility</u> for their own learning and actions, and for the learning of others. Through the Honor Roll, Critter Island experiences, the nature trail, and other student-directed projects, the students assume leadership roles as they learn and teach others about the school and broader community. By <u>shifting the responsibility</u> for planning and performing, caring for and demonstrating, leading, and teaching to the students, Mr. Waszak is conveying a belief that they can manage these actions with effort and preparation. Understanding them developmentally, he also provides a safety net of support and chance for recovery. Mr. Waszak's classroom management reflects a skillful <u>balancing between expectation, opportunity, and encouragement.</u>	*Reader's Response:* How can I use these ideas in my own teaching?

5

Making the Physical Environment a Partner

The teachers in the two case studies in Chapter 5 use the physical environment strategically and systematically to facilitate both student movement and learning. From meticulously labeled cabinets and supply shelves to a synchronized scheme of color, these teachers capitalize on the resources of classroom space and material objects. With careful design, orchestration, and communication, each classroom flows with utmost efficiency. For each teacher, the physical environment of the classroom assumes the persona of a symbolic teacher assistant—a true *partner* in the young adolescent students' learning.

In Case Study 8, Angela Morris, an art teacher for grades six through eight at Eastern Guilford Middle School, juggles multiple sections of this six-week elective. Without physical organization she couldn't manage the flow of students in and out, the sorting and re-sorting of materials and supplies, and the changeover in instructional content from one grade level to the next. A tidy system of work folders, designated student assistants, labeled shelves and cabinets, multiple designs and models, and ample supplies enables the learning activity in Ms. Morris's classroom to flow seamlessly.

In Case Study 9, Jodi Hofberg's management plan revolves around three colors. A sixth grade mathematics and science teacher at Turrentine Middle School in the Alamance-Burlington Schools, Ms. Hofberg attributes her passion for color to ten years as an elementary teacher. Folders and portfolios, board assignments, and manipulative containers are color coded in blue, red, and green to simplify the physical management of the three blocks she teaches.

"THIS IS THEIR SPACE . . . NOT MY ROOM"

Case Study 8

When students enter Ms. Morris's art classroom, they know exactly what to do. Portfolio-sized work folders, each creatively decorated with block letter initials, await collection from a center table near the front whiteboard. Following

> When students enter Ms. Morris's art classroom, they know exactly what to do.

several friendly "Good mornings," Ms. Morris's crisp voice can be heard: "If you need resource materials from the back, you have two minutes to get what you need and return to your seat." This class of eighth graders is working on drafts for thematic maze drawings. One girl has selected a Pooh Bear design, and several guys are using sports images. Ms. Morris instructs the students to take these drafts out of the work folders and continue. "Please take time with your mazes. Use your imagination," she reminds. She suggests adding a honey pot to the Pooh design.

Ms. Morris takes roll by checking the names on any folders remaining on the front table. At each student desk is a black plastic tray that holds common art supplies—colored pencils, crayons, glue sticks, and rulers. As the thirteen-year-olds get settled, light talk about football can be heard from two boys' tables near the long windows. Two of the students are in wheelchairs. Ms. Morris reminds the class that they will need to trace the drafts onto white paper for the final product. A couple of students get a sheet of this white paper from the back table and position it against the glass door by the teacher's desk for better tracing light. Ms. Morris tells another student to "please cap that glue stick."

The atmosphere in Ms. Morris's sun-filled art room is calm and relaxed on this morning in late September. The student work tables are arranged in groups of two in rows facing the whiteboard. On a counter that runs the length of the side wall near the door are boxes labeled "Yarn," "Letters for tracing," and "Scissors." Paint trays share space with large art books, pictures, and a vase of artificial flowers. Cabinets at the back of the room, each labeled with a grade and block number, open onto large shelves. On one of these shelves, Ms. Morris will deposit the stack of student work folders gathered at the end of this class. From another shelf, she will get another set for the next group's arrival. Several other shelves in the back are designated for construction paper and design sample storage.

Ms. Morris's classroom is located at the beginning of the sixth grade hall facing the central hub area of the Eastern Guilford Middle School in Greensboro, North Carolina. It is a relatively large room with the side door opening onto a patio area. Over the classroom door, just inside, is a poster conveying that "What we see depends mainly on what we're looking for." Another poster at the back reads, "The willingness to do creates the ability to do." Bulletin boards showcase colorful student-scaled drawings and multimedia art projects. A word wall of art terms rises above the whiteboard. On the board an agenda appears to be more of a list of cognitive objectives than the typically seen itemized activities:

Grade 6

Describe Roman Art.

Describe music. Define portrait.

Grade 7

What are three kinds of balance?

Explain complementary and analogous colors.

Define symmetry. Describe positive/negative.

Grade 8

Explain value scale.

Shadow? Reflection?

Define medium, mean.

All sixth, seventh, and eighth graders at Eastern Guilford take Ms. Morris's nine-week, forty-minute art elective during the course of the school year. Eighth graders, the veterans, are familiar with the classroom, the procedures, and Ms. Morris's expectations. When the sixth graders enter the art room for the first time, however, they need to be acclimated carefully to the physical layout of the room, the routines, and the anticipated flow of movement. Ms. Morris devotes a good amount of class time in the beginning making certain these expectations are communicated and understood. The activity in a sixth grade class as electives alternate is different, as the following scenario reveals.

> Ms. Morris devotes a good amount of class time in the beginning making certain these expectations are communicated and understood.

It's mid-November and the first day of election rotation. The sixth graders, seated by pairs at the work tables, direct their attention to Ms. Morris at the front of the room. Placed on each desk is an empty, unnamed, unadorned blue folder. "Are you comfortable? Can you see the board? Can you see me?" questions Ms. Morris. The eleven-year-olds indicate their satisfaction in unison. "If you're comfortable, then this is your assigned seat from here on. This is where I expect to see you." Ms. Morris calls the roll orally, asking the students to forgive her beforehand for any mispronunciations. The class, representative of the school system's changing demographics, is nearly 25 percent Latino.

Referring to a list of Expectations posted beside the whiteboard, Ms. Morris begins her explanation of the class proceedings: "Be here every day and on time. That's the first. Class starts at 11:35, so I'd like to get started by 11:38 with pencils sharpened. Fair enough? Number 2 is to bring a pencil." Ms. Morris pauses to make sure the eleven-year-olds are listening, "What time should you be in your seat?" Following a correct response, she continues, "I expect that, even if I'm not here. I need to count on you to handle that." The third expectation is to sit in assigned seats, and the fourth is to show respect. "Talk nicely like coming into one of your own homes. Listen when I talk. I won't talk all of the time," she smiles. For the fourth expectation, "to work quietly," Ms. Morris clarifies, "You can talk but keep the volume down." For the last one, "clean up your work area," she simply adds, "Don't blame your partner."

The orientation continues with a tour of the classroom's physical space. Ms. Morris directs the sixth graders' attention to the side of the room near the door. "You can use the computer only after work is finished. The sink and paper towels are for cleaning the work areas. The paper cutter is not to be touched! The supplies are for your daily use," she directs, as she makes her way to the back of the classroom. Ms. Morris points to a cabinet that is labeled "6–3" (sixth grade, third period) as the location for this class's folder storage. Beside the windows near her desk, Ms. Morris pauses at the glass door opening onto the patio. She allows that the students may use the panes for tracing but is quick to add, "The door locks behind you, so don't fool around." At the front of the room, Ms. Morris warns that the "very warm" kiln room is for her use only, pointing to the nearby fire alarm to underline the restriction. When she calls for questions, only one boy asks, "Which way is the bathroom from this class?"

With the visual expedition around the classroom complete, Ms. Morris instructs the sixth graders to take out a sheet of paper. On the whiteboard she writes, "Art Note Page," and explains that art has basic vocabulary just as English. She refers to the word wall and begins an introduction to the seven elements of art, the first of which is line. With brisk pace, the students brainstorm different kinds of lines—curvy, broken, diagonal, zigzag, wide, thin, double, thick, parallel. Ms. Morris records these ideas on the whiteboard and the sixth graders take notes.

Next, the students are asked to put the notes in the blue folder for another activity. For application, Ms. Morris instructs them to trace the first initial of their names on a small sheet of white paper using the assorted sizes of block letters spread out on the back table. She calls the students back to the table by rows and requests that they pass the letters among each other as they are used. Each white letter tracing will be glued in the center of the blue folders, and the surrounding area decorated creatively with as many different kinds of lines as the students can incorporate. This task will individualize their work folders for the upcoming weeks of the elective.

While the sixth graders work, Ms. Morris circulates, collects, and passes letters, offers comments, and practices the students' names: "That looks neat, Jon. Very nice, Nadia. Who has used a wavy line? Try to use all kinds. It's OK to repeat the same line. Outline the letters so we can see them well. Be sure to glue the edges of the white paper down carefully." When one girl laments that she has "messed up," Ms. Morris gives her an eraser from a box on her desk. The students move back and forth freely, getting markers from the supply buckets and testing them. They use the glue sticks and pencils at their desks unless anything needs to be replenished.

When the large television monitor at the front right corner of the room indicates 12:17, Ms. Morris asks the students to stop, pass the work folders back to the person behind them, return all pencils, markers, and glue, and to clean up. A minute later, the work areas are surprisingly clean and the folders stacked on the center table. Ms. Morris, seated on the front stool, asks a few quick review questions about the seven design elements and her classroom expectations. As the monitor shows 12:20, Ms. Morris dismisses the class row by row. No bells ring at Eastern Guilford; however, all teachers and students maintain a close watch over time.

> Instead of a laundry list of management strategies, she tries to determine what the students need to help them to learn.

A graduate of East Carolina University, Ms. Morris holds a bachelor of science in art with a K–12 licensure. She has seventeen years of teaching experience at the elementary or middle school level. She attributes much of her classroom management effectiveness as "instinctive," or to use a term from a recent reading workshop she attended, "unconsciously competent." Instead of a laundry list of management strategies, she tries to determine what the students need to help them to learn. One year, for instance, she noticed that her art students were having difficulty staying on task for large blocks of time. In response, she began to break her instruction into ten- to fifteen-minute segments, cueing students ahead of the time when they would stop and move to the next activity. She knew that the students liked this change, though she didn't fully realize the value until she, as a mentor, observed a new teacher having difficulty with student on-task behavior. She suggested that the teacher think about the strategy.

> Ms. Morris believes that young adolescents need freedom to explore and create in order to learn and grow. At the same time, she knows that they need limitations.

Ms. Morris believes that young adolescents need freedom to explore and create in order to learn and grow. At the same time, she knows that they need limitations. She sees middle school as a time of transitional growth, when students stretch themselves and test these limits. "For most students, this is the way they learn. As they grow, they learn what is acceptable behavior and what is not," she explains. Her perception of her own classroom management style parallels these beliefs about young adolescents and their learning needs: "Sometimes I think my style is very relaxed. However, expectations are established at the beginning so the atmosphere is one of freedom with limitation. Everyone understands and accepts the limits," she indicates. She confesses that she doesn't like to repeat herself, so "I get it all out on the first day. Students hate lectures, so they don't mind."

> She starts building relationships with students from the first day by finding out who they are and what they enjoy.

As evident in the time Ms. Morris takes to introduce new students to the procedures unique to her art room, she genuinely wants them to feel they belong there. She starts building relationships with students from the first day by finding out who they are and what they enjoy. Ms. Morris is also willing to let her students relate to her as a person. On a small front table, among several interesting items for the students to sketch, is a pair of platform shoes. When a sixth grade boy asks about the shoes, Ms. Morris tells him that she wore them as homecoming queen. "That was a time when you weren't even born," she laughs.

Ms. Morris firmly believes that teachers should show respect for students as individuals and to treat them accordingly. She interacts with her young adolescents in art with verbal politeness, and in response to this attitude, their respect is reciprocated. At one point during a class, her back turned, she addresses a student behind her in a calm, matter-of-fact voice, "Anton, getting a lot done over there?" The boy responds, "Yes, ma'am."

Ms. Morris understands young adolescents and their developmental challenges, and she admits that sometimes this requires a good deal of patience and forgiveness. She is adamant about giving second chances, and her policy for accepting late work is indicative. She issues computer-generated interim reports that update the students on the status of their work completed by the set due dates. These reports must be taken home and signed by parents. According to Ms. Morris, if the student is given a zero on an assignment on the interim report, it could mean one of several things: (a) They did not do it, (b) it's lost somewhere in the room, (c) it simply hasn't been turned in, or (d) it's Ms. Morris's mistake. Students are given the chance to change their status before leaving class or to bring in the completed work within a reasonable length of time. One student discovered that his perspective drawing had slipped out of his work folder in the cabinet. The zero was corrected.

> There will always be someone who will misbehave. Thus teachers have to be physically and mentally ready for almost anything.

Even with the strong physical organization, clear expectations, and opportunities for redemption, Ms. Morris recognizes realistically that young adolescents need to be watched and reminded. She notes that there will always be someone who will misbehave. Thus teachers have to be physically and mentally ready for almost anything. The interim reports, for example, caused some stir one day when a few of the eighth grade boys began comparing notes and exchanging jibes. Ms. Morris quickly stepped in: "Excuse me. I don't have anybody in here called an idiot." She's also firm about the students' showing respect to her when she is talking, and will correct any student who is not following this expectation. Students are furthermore expected to be where they're expected to be. To an eighth grade boy who stopped at a peer's desk, Ms. Morris states, "I appreciate your working at your own desk. You'll get a chance to go through everybody's maze." To another she addresses, "Why are you back here? Are you getting anything done today?"

> Ms. Morris's purposeful use of the physical space facilitates the young adolescents' movement, activity, and learning.

During the transitional time for cleanup and preparation to change classes, Ms. Morris can often be heard saying a simple chant-response: "If you hear my voice, clap once. If you hear my voice, clap twice." With this cue, the students get quiet, and she is able to give the final directions: "Push your chairs in and have a good day."

Ms. Morris's purposeful use of the physical space facilitates the young adolescents' movement, activity, and learning. Her art classroom, nevertheless, is much more than a system of work folders, accessible shelves, and ready supplies. Her class is a student-friendly environment, and students are trusted with its care. In forty-minute turnovers, Ms. Morris's sixth, seventh, and eighth graders come and go, opening and closing the short intervals of instructional time. She sincerely wants the numerous students she teaches each year to feel a personal sense of belonging, responsibility, and ownership as they enter and exit for the elective. According to Ms. Morris, "It's their space . . . not my classroom."

IF IT'S WRITTEN IN BLUE . . .

Case Study 9

When Jodi Hofberg grew weary of spending valuable instructional time helping her sixth graders learn to open the locks on their lockers, she tried a new strategy. On parent open house night at the beginning of the school year, she issued the locks and combinations so that parents could go with the students into the hallway and assist. Not only did this simple change of procedure save time (and a headache!), it also improved parent attendance. As a sixth grade teacher at Turrentine Middle, a Grades 6

Color-coded management . . .

through 8 school in Burlington, North Carolina, Ms. Hofberg realizes that the eleven-year-olds who come to her class each year have a big step to make. From the more protective environment of elementary school, these students must shift toward being able to take care of themselves. In accordance, she continually seeks ways to ease this transition. Color-coded management is one of the most effective methods she's found to get and keep her sixth graders organized for learning. Through this approach, she hopes that they will begin to develop their own organizational style, "especially the boys," she adds with a smile.

The gregarious Ms. Hofberg stands at the door greeting students for Block II math class. She comments on a female student's new hairstyle and calls to another to "move it on up the hall." The sixth graders enter, go immediately to the table in front of the overhead, pick a warm-up handout (three grade-level-six problem-solving tasks), and begin work. The desk tables are arranged in seven squares of four, with pairs of students facing each other.

When Ms. Hofberg steps back into the room, the students are quiet and working. She places one of the warm-ups on an empty desk, presumably for a late student, and begins to circulate and respond to raised hands. A "Good Work" sticker, worth one point on their math grade, is awarded each student for starting on time. A carryover from ten years as an elementary teacher, this point system works for Ms. Hofberg and the transitioning eleven-year-olds. She admits that she uses it sparingly, however, and only at the beginning of the year.

Ms. Hofberg calls time and asks a student named Patrick to go up to the overhead, write his solution to the math tickler, and explain his work.

Student-Led Demonstration

Anyone using the overhead gets to sit in Ms. Hofberg's comfortable deck chair. The boy carries his warm-up sheet to the front and begins to write as he talks. At one point, Ms. Hofberg, who is standing in the back, interjects to the class, "What do we call that . . . farthest place value from the end of the problem?" A student answers, "Front end estimation," and Ms. Hofberg tells Patrick to "keep going." She leans over and helps a student with the placement of a zero and comma: "There you go!" she praises. The sixth graders check and correct their work. A student named Erica is asked to read the next problem, which deals with inverse numbers. "Basically the opposites," Ms. Hofberg explains. She raises the overhead screen to uncover a hint to the third challenge.

One glance around Ms. Hofberg's classroom reveals the inescapable logic of the color-coded organization plan. Block I is blue, Block II is red, and Block III is green. The scheme is carried out on a Classroom Duties chart, the homework assignments written on the side of the whiteboard, the folders where Ms. Hofberg keeps grades, and the students' homework folders and individual work portfolios. Against the row of windows are large crates of corresponding colors that hold supplies and materials for each block. Instead of looking for "Block 1," she says, "the students look for their color."

Ms. Hofberg admits that a lot of time goes into the initial setup, but that the simplicity of organization that the system provides is worth it. "At this point in their development," she justifies with reference to the young adolescents, "*less is better* for them. Some have never even written down a homework assignment." The color-coded plan enables the students to focus their attention on learning, and Ms. Hofberg can concentrate on what she enjoys the most—teaching! Block II's math lesson, now beginning, is a good example of her instructional skill.

With the warm-up over, Ms. Hofberg asks the sixth graders to put the checked papers in their blue work folders and to take out their math journals. These small booklets were assembled by Ms. Hofberg from stapled notebook paper and construction paper as a cover. The students have journals for each of the four areas of the state's sixth grade math curriculum. Ms. Hofberg sits in the deck chair at the overhead, her marker poised over the acetate ready to give notes. "What do we do with a new concept?" she inquires as she begins writing the word "Exponent" (see Figure 5.1). A student responds, "Put it in a bubble," and Ms. Hofberg encircles the word with squiggly lines. "I see some people with journals not open yet. I want you to stay with me."

Teacher Modeling

Ms. Hofberg asks what exponents look like, and calls on a student who needs to "pass" to another. Underneath the word, Ms. Hofberg writes "Ex. 4^2" and labels the two parts as "Base" and "Exponent." Below she bullets and defines each term, talking aloud as she writes. "Four to the power of 2," she reiterates, and asks the student to repeat it. She asks a boy, "What's going to let

Figure 5.1 Math Notes

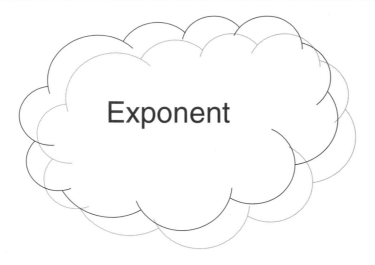

Ex. 4^2

- Base = a factor that gets repeated!
- Exponent = the number that tells you how many times to repeat the base.

me know how many times to repeat?" To his response, "Whatever the number," she probes, "Whatever *what* number?" The student responds to her satisfaction, "Exponent."

Ms. Hofberg continues with this interaction of writing, explaining, questioning, and probing for specificity. "Listen to my question. What is another way to say it?" she asks, and writes the student's response on the transparency: "Four to the 2nd power." "Tell me one more way," Ms. Hofberg ventures, and reminds the class of the previous week's discussion of area. She writes a third way, "Four squared," for the sixth graders to copy into their math journals.

For practice, the students use small individual whiteboards, markers, and erasers, which are distributed from the supplies box by a designated table person. They write the answer to Ms. Hofberg's first question: "Three to the 4th power." The sixth graders hold up their boards to show their work, and Ms. Hofberg holds up the correct board, indicating, "It should look like this." She continues, "All right, erase for the next one. Write big enough so we can all see," and reminds, "Write, close marker, then hold up your board when I say to. I'm saying them in different ways. Check your notes. What's another way to say this?" The brisk pace continues. "I'm seeing more and more of you getting them right," she comments.

Ongoing Assessment

Ms. Hofberg stops the practice session for the next set of overhead notes. Using the previous example, she writes "Ex. $4^2 = 4 \times 4$" on the overhead and reviews that the base number gets repeated according to the exponent. She shows them how to write the operation using a small dot, larger than a decimal, smiling, "We're sixth graders. We love shortcuts." Ms. Hofberg demonstrates two other examples and asks the students to tell her how to write out the factoring. The small whiteboards come out for more practice, and students write the exponential form as she calls it out. This go-round, however, they add the factoring underneath. Again Ms. Hofberg circulates and checks responses as the students hold up their boards on cue. "If you don't feel comfortable using dots, it's OK to use x's," she allows.

More overhead note taking begins with Ms. Hofberg's announcement, "Alert! An important math rule that you need to memorize: Any number to zero power is always equal to 1." She writes this rule on the overhead with a star by it and adds two examples. The students follow suit in their math journals. The last segment of the math lesson involves finding values. On the overhead, Ms. Hofberg writes, "How to write an exponent in standard form," and encircles the phrase with the familiar squiggly line. Using the example 4^3, she verbalizes as she writes, "Four times 4 equals 16, 16 times 4 equals . . ." She stresses, "Never multiply the base and the exponent. *Never.*" A few more overhead examples follow as Ms. Hofberg calls on students to explain the operations as she writes. She asks a few more probing questions and stops with the directions, "After lunch, we'll do some independent work."

Ms. Hofberg is a member of a two-teacher sixth grade team named the Voyagers. She teaches math and science, and her colleague teaches language arts and social studies. Together the two teachers manage the behavior of the Voyager Team students through a system of rights and responsibilities. What is not an acceptable action is coded and tracked on Ms. Hofberg's Uh-Oh List, a computer-generated spreadsheet bearing each student's name. A few of the unacceptable behaviors include T = Tardy, UP = Unprepared, D = Disruptive/ Disrespectful, and BO = Blurting Out (students love this one!). Consequences for misbehaviors range on a continuum from Number 1, a verbal warning with the student's name on the board beside the coded action, to Number 6, a referral to the principal's office. This six-point plan of action places much responsibility for behavioral management on the young adolescents, parents, and classroom teachers. Before the sixth step, teachers are expected to contact and conference with the individual student's parents.

Shared Responsibility With Students and Parents

Each week on Fridays, Ms. Hofberg and her teammate send home the Voyager Team Weekly Checklist, which must be read, signed by students and parents, and returned the following Monday. This report keeps caretakers informed about recurring concerns that can range from cheating or dress code violations to being unprepared with needed materials for class. Ms. Hofberg explains that each sixth grader is given a locker information sheet that specifies what items are needed for each class, so there's no excuse for coming unprepared! On this checklist is also a place to mark "Your child had a great week!" next to a happy

> Fairness is important to them and your own consistency.

face. The checklist helps during parent conferences, Ms. Hofberg attests, if she needs to justify students' grades on report cards.

By being assertive, consistent, and open about her expectations and consequences, Ms. Hofberg knows she helps her sixth graders adjust more readily to the middle school environment. She understands that the young adolescents need to know they are treated fairly. "Fairness is important to them and your own consistency," she notes. She has also discovered after three years teaching this age of students that "the less you say, the better." She explains, "They know right from wrong and you don't want to give them a chance to give you an excuse." If you've clearly discussed what you expect and why this is important to classroom learning, and if you can be relied upon for fair enforcement, according to Ms. Hofberg, "no further explanation is generally needed."

Ms. Hofberg additionally enforces strict guidelines concerning classroom movement, such as pencil sharpening and throwing away trash. A system that has worked very well for movement during activities, transitions, and classroom jobs is the simple coding of tables. At the top right corner of each of the seven sets of desks, she has taped a number, to designate table cluster and a letter to denote individual desk. If Ms. Hofberg wants one person at a table to help distribute or clear materials, such as during the math lesson on exponents, she simply indicates, "People in A seat, please collect the math board, markers, and erasers and put them back in the right box" (see Figure 5.2).

Figure 5.2 Table Task Designations

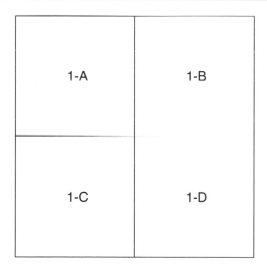

A System for Movement

If Ms. Hofberg's sixth graders understand and follow classroom procedures, whether related to the color-coded organization setup or her expectations for movement and proper behavior, she feels she can allow them flexibility and choice in their academic learning. The day the class began trading on the stock market is a good example. An early morning in mid-November finds the sixth graders positioned over computer keyboards, trying to follow the directions on a green handout. Ms. Hofberg has put a link to a simulated stock market WebQuest on the school's site, and students are in various stages of logging on. "You are about to enter the world of e-stock and trading," the computer screen reads. Each student had been given 10,000 shares to invest in e-stocks of their choice. "Your goal is be a wise investor. Research your stock picks before you make a purchase," the directions on the WebQuest indicate. Scattered around on tables among the computers are current newspapers.

The class will play this free simulation game, during school hours only, from mid-November until mid-May. Ms. Hofberg's management plan for using the laptop computers, which are rolled into the classroom on a cart, is to assign each student the same one each time. If a student fails to plug an individual computer back in correctly, there will be no power the next day. The sixth graders have been given specific instructions about the computers' handling and care.

In a previous lesson, the eleven-year-olds had checked newspapers to find the price per share of several well-known company stocks. For real-world practice in using decimal points, the students had calculated each stock's value or, as they learned, its price for buying and selling purposes. They had also self-selected five stocks and performed the same calculation (see Figure 5.3). The current day's task is to track the stocks' fluctuations to decide if they want to invest, continue to follow a particular stock, or research other options. For a preliminary activity, Ms. Hofberg had discussed the concept of owning stocks and had introduced the term *dividends* as divided or "shared" profits. They also discussed the notion of selling stocks for gains and what it meant to buy on margin. The young adolescents' excitement is evident in their chatter.

Figure 5.3 Stock Market Task Grid

Price per Share Value

Directions: Select five companies of your choice and figure the value if you were to purchase the number of shares given.

Name of Company	Number of Shares	Price per Share	Value
1			
2			
3			
4			
5			

SOURCE: Used with permission from J. Hofberg, Turrentine Middle School, Burlington, NC, in *Managing the Adolescent Classroom: Lessons From Outstanding Teachers,* by Glenda Beamon Crawford. (2004). Corwin Press, Thousand Oaks, CA. www.corwinpress.com.

Ms. Hofberg confesses that she is as excited about the stock market simulation as the eleven-year-olds. Several students who have been unmotivated by more traditional teaching methods "really get into this," she indicates, adding, "and parents *love* it." She moves among the tables, assists with technical difficulties, and helps the sixth graders who are having a problem with logging on to the school Web site to access the simulation. "Go to Set Quote," Ms. Hofberg instructs, "and see what it is today." She points out that they are not day traders but rather stock trackers. While some of the students may make an initial investment and follow it, others might make several transactions over the course of the simulation. Each student's account earns 4 percent interest, and Ms. Hofberg charges $15 per trade as stockbroker.

Authentic Learning Engagement

Much too quickly for the sixth graders, the period ends and they have to get ready to leave for an elective. Ms. Hofberg turns out the overhead lights momentarily and the students get quiet. "Thank you," she says, and continues with directions for shutting down the computers. "Remember what has to happen to the screen? It has to go black." She helps the students file the computers back on the cart in the numbered places. The young adolescents ready their materials to leave.

QUESTIONS FOR CONSIDERATION AND RESPONSE

1. How does Ms. Morris use physical space and time advantageously for classroom management?

Ms. Morris's <u>intentional organization</u> of the art room's physical space (labeled cabinets, supplies stations, table materials, designs and models, use of whiteboard, word walls) enables her to manage with efficiency the frequent turnover of students and levels. The personalized folder system assists in managing individual work while clearly shifting responsibility for maintenance to the students. If work is missing or overdue, they simply locate or complete it. The folder serves as a physical connection between Ms. Morris and the young adolescents. This use of physical surroundings facilitates the flow of movement and transitions among various tasks and between sections, and it also helps	*Reader's Response:* How can I use these ideas in my own teaching?

(Continued)

(Continued)

Ms. Morris make maximal use of instructional time. The organization plan furthermore serves as a classroom road map that gives students the <u>needed structure developmentally for social interaction and movement.</u> Once the young adolescents are acclimated to the plan and understand Ms. Morris's expectations for their involvement in it, the classroom space becomes a symbolic partner in facilitating both learning and behavioral management.	
2. What is the significance of the title "This Is Their Space . . . Not My Room"? In what ways is the atmosphere of the art room developmentally responsive to the young adolescent students?	
Ms. Morris's motivation in establishing a physical management system, to maximize instructional time and guide classroom activity, is her hope that students would care about and <u>take ownership</u> in its operation. Young adolescents respond favorably to a learning environment where they are treated as individuals who can be trusted to manage themselves. They also respond well to the security of <u>knowing where the boundaries are</u> placed to guide their tentative development of self-discipline behavior. The physical surroundings could be likened to props in the stage production of Ms. Morris's classroom script, though she knows it may take some dress rehearsals and firm reminders for the show to go as anticipated! She allows the <u>freedom for students to demonstrate that they can be responsible caretakers,</u> yet she provides the <u>necessary structure of predictability</u> and consistency. Within this atmosphere of belief, acceptance, and expectancy, the young adolescents appear, for the most part, to carry their role in the performance. Accordingly, the students make the classroom their own and Ms. Morris can relax a little and enjoy being in the play.	*Reader's Response:* How can I use these ideas in my own teaching?

(Continued)

3. How does Ms. Hofberg make the physical environment a partner in her sixth grade classroom?	
In a similar management style, Ms. Hofberg strategically uses the physical trappings of the classroom to facilitate movement and to organize for instruction. Her choice of structure is color, and she uses it to keep up with the daily agendas, portfolios, papers, homework assignments, and supplies of three blocks. While the color scheme helps Ms. Hofberg manage daily activity, it also provides a transitional aid for the sixth graders who are trying to adjust to the more complex environment of middle school. The color-coded system provides an element of security for the students, <u>a pathway for managing time, multiple tasks, supplementary materials, and personal work.</u> An easy visual, color also gives each block an identity associated with that particular group. Ms. Hofberg admits the initial setup of this management system is time-consuming, but the longer-term benefit is like having an assistant in the classroom.	*Reader's Response:* How can I use these ideas in my own teaching?
4. What instructional and other management strategies does Ms. Hofberg use that help the sixth graders transition to middle school?	
Ms. Hofberg views the responsibility of teaching math and science to the sixth graders and <u>helping them transition</u> to middle school as equally important and interrelated challenges. Beyond operating locks and remembering combinations, the new middle schoolers must adapt to less supervision of movement and an increased expectation for personal time management. Having personally made the transition from teaching fifth grade to sixth, Ms. Hofberg is aware of the differences between school levels. As discussed in Question 3, she has found that color helps. Other transitional strategies include the <u>inclusion of parents</u> in the mastery of lock manipulation (which also	*Reader's Response:* How can I use these ideas in my own teaching?

(Continued)

(Continued)

builds community!), the <u>use of physical tools</u> to assist with learning and self-organization (portfolios, graphic organizers, math notebooks, slates), <u>personal modeling</u> through demonstration and verbalization of thought processes (math note taking), and a <u>behavioral management system</u> that clarifies and communicates specific expectations to students and parents regularly. Young adolescents need these bridges, or scaffolds, to help them make the steps toward more self-directed learning and personal management.	
5. How does Ms. Hofberg motivate and maximize learning? Why is a high level of engagement a successful classroom management strategy?	
Similar to the teachers in the previous case studies, Ms. Hofberg motivates through meaningful, academically challenging instruction that encourages <u>social interaction</u> and <u>student choice.</u> Following the stock market on personal computers and making <u>decisions that simulate those made in real life</u> are engaging to young adolescents who seek greater autonomy and independence. Ms. Hofberg also manages by a <u>variety of tasks</u> (note taking, slate assessment, independent application) and <u>frequent and well-monitored transitions</u> between segments. She <u>involves the students actively</u> and in ways that build their self-confidence (problems projected on the overhead and verbalization). Her verbal interaction with the young adolescents is fast-paced and skillful, yet she continually makes certain that no student is frustrated or confused through her questioning and other <u>informal assessments.</u> No time is wasted, the tasks are worthwhile, and the students are helped to achieve. As a <u>positive environment</u> for the young adolescents' development of healthy self-esteem and competence, Ms. Hofberg's class is a win-win experience.	*Reader's Response:* How can I use these ideas in my own teaching?

6

Knowing What Works for You

The two case studies in Chapter 6 feature teachers who differ widely in teaching style, personality, subject area, and years of experience. Each, however, knows what is necessary to facilitate learning in her particular classroom setting. They also know what they *personally* need from students to make it happen.

Joyce Covington, certified in Family and Consumer Science (6–12), teaches an elective called Career Decisions/Life Skills at Hawfields Middle School in the Alamance-Burlington Schools in Mebane, North Carolina. A twenty-seven-year veteran with teaching experiences from fourth to twelfth grade, Ms. Covington manages a complex classroom environment of hands-on learning centers with calm reserve. She spends considerable time initially prepping her heterogeneously grouped classes of sixth and seventh graders about procedures for movement and safety. Her classes consequently run with smooth efficiency as groups of students rotate from one work station to another.

Patricia Berge, in her third year of teaching eighth grade science at McDougle Middle School in the Chapel Hill-Carrboro Schools, has a contrasting classroom management style that suits her just fine. Small groups of students lean together over desks and spill out into the wide hallway to conduct physics lab experiments. Ms. Berge can be seen walking among or kneeling next to the sprawled bodies of thirteen-year-olds. What might appear to a passerby as noisy interaction, however, is transformed into student-led presentations that indicate sophisticated content understanding and analysis.

PROCEED WITH CAUTION

Case Study 10

Understanding procedure is important in Ms. Covington's Career Decisions/Life Skills classes at Hawfields Middle. At a given time, seven groups of students might be seen rotating through the ten centers around the large classroom baking cookies, sewing on fabric, or learning about cosmetic makeovers. When students arrive for the elective, they know to wait in the hallway against the wall. Why? That's the traffic pattern for the school building during class change. A new group of sixth or seventh graders stand outside Ms. Covington's class every forty-five minutes. When invited in, they know to go directly to their assigned seats to await the familiar greeting, "Good morning, Life Skills."

Clear Communication of Procedure

Once inside the classroom, Ms. Covington's students are familiar with other procedures. They know that if the classroom phone rings, they should remain quiet: It's generally the office. They also don't need to say, "Phone's ringing," since everyone can hear it. They know how to open the file cabinet properly to retrieve the digital camera or the baby monitor. They know they can borrow a pencil from the cup on the overhead as long as it is returned at the end of class. They know that the colored pencils are for their use but that it disappoints Ms. Covington when these get broken. They know that rolling or tapping pencils on desks is distracting when anyone is talking. They know they can access the sewing materials when working in that center, or they can go and get glue, markers, scissors, and rulers, as needed for another station, without asking permission. Ms. Covington's students also know that they should *not* spit in the sink.

———————————————
A visual tour . . .
———————————————

In the initial days of the election rotation, Ms. Covington takes a new group of students on a visual tour around the perimeter of her class, explaining what is found in each area and what is expected from them. The students respectfully follow her with their heads and eyes as she points out where particular supplies are located and which ones are necessary for which activities. Ms. Covington prefaces the tour with, "The more you listen, the faster I can talk," and she questions them periodically to be sure they are absorbing the information. By moving from center to center, Ms. Covington is also giving the young adolescents a brief overview of the learning experiences they can anticipate during the six-week course.

Taking time for a visual tour is important to the flow of activity movement that Ms. Covington expects. With the variety of hands-on centers around the classroom, it is important that the young adolescents know the procedure within each, especially related to safety. During the span of the elective, students are allowed to choose to work in three of the available ten stations. The students know exactly what to do because the procedure is clear: Enter quietly, place book bags in the front of the classroom beneath the whiteboard, be seated in the assigned seat, and listen attentively as Ms. Covington takes attendance and gives general instructions for the day's activities.

As Ms. Covington reads the center's name, one person in that group comes forward to get the center folder while others move to the designated area to begin gathering necessary materials. A notebook at each center contains complete directions for the center's activity. Four minutes before class change, Ms. Covington alerts the students for cleanup time. They return materials to the proper place, move back to their original seats, and wait to be dismissed. No class time is lost.

Getting to know the procedures for movement and center activity is a concerted class effort. Ms. Covington hands out a computer-typed handout accompanied by a fill-in-the-blank worksheet that she also makes into an overhead transparency. Individual students come up to the projector, write in the correct answer, and read the particular expectation aloud. At any time during subsequent class periods, if the procedures are not followed, activities are stopped and the course of action is relearned.

> At any time during subsequent class periods, if the procedures are not followed, activities are stopped and the course of action is relearned.

Once this modus operandi groundwork is laid, Ms. Covington's classes move smoothly and she is free to rotate, monitor, and assist, from center to center. When disruptive behavior does occur, however, she has another process that is also well-known to the students. If changing a seating arrangement does not solve the problem and if a private student conference to discuss the matter also fails, they know their parents will be contacted at work or home. Ms. Covington is fortunate to have a telephone with an outside line in the classroom as a direct link for computer technical

> Behavior is different when you sit.

assistance. Next to this phone she keeps a list of all her students' parents' names and phone numbers. She simply connects with the parent and hands the phone over to the student to "tell what you're doing right now." Then she talks. According to Ms. Covington, this procedure generally solves the problem.

Managing the activity of ten different learning centers is a highly physical feat. This veteran, however, does so energetically, calmly, and with physical presence. "Stand up, move, get next to them—it works!" Ms. Covington recommends to anyone. "Behavior is different when you sit." Respect is expected and shown in the way she and the students interact. They are patient when she is helping in another center, and they know that when her back is turned, she can still distinguish voices. "I can feel activities of the room without actually looking at them," she admits.

> When students operate within the realm of her expectations, they are free to manage their own activity.

Procedures are important for the maintenance of the complex environment of machinery and appliances, but the impetus behind Ms. Covington's procedures for movement and behavior goes beyond mere physical management. When students operate within the realm of her expectations, they are free to manage their own activity. While the success of the plan depends on the students' willingness to follow her agenda, when they do, they become empowered to take personal responsibility. Ms. Covington provides an Achievement Checklist for all students, clipped to the front of their center work. As they complete the items listed, they are expected to ask her to sign the checklist. This individual organizational strategy works well for the students.

Personal management is also evident in Ms. Covington's grading system, which encompasses students' academic work and participation. Each student begins with a full participation credit of 100 points. Points are deducted for actions not consistent with class procedures. These actions include horseplay, name-calling, arguing with classmates, excessive talking, being out of an assigned center, not taking care of materials, not staying on task, and not cleaning up center materials. Participation grades, taken weekly, are affected by the manner in which Ms. Covington's students choose to behave. Knowing these students' developmental nature, however, she builds in many opportunities for social interaction, choice, variety, and movement. She admittedly tries to stay in tune with the students' needs as she helps them take more personal control over their academic learning and social behavior.

> She builds in many opportunities for social interaction, choice, variety, and movement.

Ms. Covington's intentional effort to establish clear procedures early pays off in the responsibility the students assume for the classroom's care. The students understand, for example, what will happen to the shears in the sewing cabinet if they are used to cut anything other than two-ply fabric. They know why they should lay out towels in the kitchen center to dry until there are enough for a full load. They are also aware of the importance of work center cleanliness: 100 students rotate through this Career Decisions/Life Skills elective daily.

> . . . relevance to the lives of the young adolescents.

Another key factor in the synchronized flow of center activity in Ms. Covington's class is content that has clear relevance to the lives of the young adolescents she teaches. In one unit, for example, the students are given pretend careers and expected to buy a house, buy a car, and pay bills with the budgeted income allotted for that career. The students also learn to sew, cook, use the computer, and participate in many other true-life skills. On the day described below, instead of rotating through centers, Ms. Covington's sixth graders will be working at individual tables. Their task is to design a personal business card for an occupation, which had been determined earlier by the random overturning of job cards. The range of options included plumber, lawyer, computer programmer, meteorologist, teacher, and mail carrier, to name a few.

Now Ms. Covington is standing at the overhead explaining the directions for the task: The students are to create a 3" × 4" business card to advertise their occupations (see Figure 6.1). The eleven-year-olds will first make a draft on notebook paper according to the specifications projected on the screen. A red star by "Your Name," she explains, indicates the only part that has to be real. In addition, the only required number is the telephone number, but the students are welcome to make up the others.

Figure 6.1   Business Card Format

Name of Business _____

Your Name _____

Address _____

Telephone Number _____

E-mail _____

Fax Number _____

Pager _____

Hours of Operation _____

Logo _____   Slogan _____   Motto _____

SOURCE: Used with permission from J. Covington, Hawfields Middle School, Mebane, NC, in *Managing the Adolescent Classroom: Lessons From Outstanding Teachers,* by Glenda Beamon Crawford. (2004). Corwin Press, Thousand Oaks, CA. www.corwinpress.com.

When a few students begin to express concern about what to name their businesses, Ms. Covington indicates to "just take notes now. Later we'll have some thinking time." Half-page laminated samples are scattered around on the students' table areas for reference. "Are you ready to pay close attention?" Ms. Covington cues. One student calls out, "What if the phone number is 1-800-GET LOST?" Calmly, Ms. Covington says, "For a business card, let's be serious," and begins to review the proper way to write an address. She displays a sample on the overhead with red lines drawn under the letters needing capitalization. A volunteer comes to the overhead to write a sample address while the other students practice at their desks. She next displays a transparency with six business card samples varying in format and orientation, and points out the differences. "You have to write very small," she advises. "Raise your hand if you have a question for the entire group. You have six minutes to work today." She reiterates the task and reminds the students to follow the guideline and check the examples.

Precisely at the end of the work period, Ms. Covington calls for cleanup time: "I need all folders stacked in the center of the table." As she circulates to collect them, she takes "a moment to talk about what we did today." She reminds them to do some "real good thinking" about their business slogans overnight. The next day, the students will finish the *real* cards "with no mistakes." Dismissal is orderly and prompt.

While Ms. Covington's classes operate efficiently and productively, her management effectiveness is additionally supported by the relationship she establishes with the young adolescent students. During the visual tour, for example, she pauses at her desk to show the students her family pictures. She shares the fact that by the end of the week, she should have a new grand-baby. Ms. Covington's first assignment is that the students write her a letter titled, "About Me." In this letter, they are asked to include information about their families, hobbies, and interests outside of school, any health concerns, their feelings about school, their attitude or outlook on life, and any special or unique qualities. They are also asked to give their first, second, and third choices in centers. Ms. Covington assures the students that she will try and honor their choices of centers, reminding them that only a limited number can be in each center at one time.

> With young adolescents, social interaction can be problematic from minute to minute.

Ms. Covington's effort to establish a positive relationship with students extends throughout the time of the elective. She acknowledges that with young adolescents, "social interaction can be problematic from minute to minute." When students are arguing, she takes them into the hallway and lets each take turns explaining what is happening. Often the instance is about a misunderstanding and can be settled. Similarly, Ms. Covington refrains from arguing with any student, allowing the student to sit quietly for a few minutes to "cool down." Her years of experience with young adolescents have shown her that "humor should be used to deal with sarcasm from adolescents in some cases. They often do not mean what they say." In a show of respect to her students, Ms. Covington's personal corrective statements are worded positively: "Be still," for example, rather than "Don't beat on your desk."

> Genuine interest she shows in their lives beyond the classroom.

Ms. Covington's personal connection with her students is further reflected in the genuine interest she shows in their lives beyond the classroom. She is deliberate about attending after-school functions at Hawfields Middle School on a regular basis and thus makes contact with students at athletic events, concerts, and band performances.

> Within this structured and positive setting, students of all abilities and socioeconomic levels have the opportunity to shine.

Perhaps the greatest benefit of Ms. Covington's procedure-based classroom is the long-term impact on the young adolescents. Within this structured and positive setting, students of all abilities and socioeconomic levels have the opportunity to shine. Whether helping to wash dishes, setting out wax paper for sugar cookies, or cutting pieces of fabric, the students realize they are making a contribution to their group. "They see that they possess day-to-day skills. . . . I can just see them glow," assesses Ms. Covington. Beyond their knowledge of nutrition, grooming, child care, cooking, career selection, and household management, these young adolescents learn about personal accountability and the need for collaboration to reach a desired goal. These real-life lessons are the most important ones that Ms. Covington's students are able to gain.

ALL WOUND UP

Case Study 11

"Today you're all going to get a brain," smiles the young teacher as she begins pulling small windup toys out of a white plastic bag and handing them to students. The scene is Ms. Berge's eighth grade science classroom at McDougle Middle School in the Chapel Hill-Carrboro Schools. "Do dry runs with your brains first," Ms. Berge instructs. "When you finish the trials, get with a partner and calculate the speed in five different intervals." The thirteen-year-olds quickly grab rulers, timers, toothpicks, and lab sheets from the green trays centered on the table desks and head for any available floor space in the large classroom. Several spill into the adjacent hallway. In less than five minutes, the classroom is transformed into a physics laboratory of sprawling adolescent bodies and bobbing windup "brains."

The eighth graders are in the second day of a lab titled All Wound Up. The task for the day, written on the whiteboard, is to finish collecting data. The next step is to calculate the negative acceleration rate of the moving object. A blue crate of calculators sits on the demonstration table at the front of the room.

As the dispersed students settle into the lab activity, Ms. Berge walks over to two girls who had been absent the previous day. She sits down on the floor beside them and demonstrates how to lay out the ruler and mark the time intervals for the data collection. "Be consistent each time. Either put the toothpick before or after the brain. If your dry run is thirty seconds, divide by 5. Count every six seconds for your trial." Ms. Berge watches as the girls do two trials. "What happens to the distance? So that means what to the speed?" she asks. With the response, "decelerates," she instructs the students to do three more trials and then fill in the data sheet. "How do you calculate speed? What is the formula?" she probes, adding, "Use your notes."

Continual Monitoring and Assessment

Ms. Berge weaves among the bodies of students, handing out small calculators. She pauses beside one group that has chosen to work on one of the flat green table surfaces. "I'd break it down," she offers, leaning over to check their work. A few minutes later, she focuses the class's attention to the front and asks a volunteer to call out the formulas for calculating speed and acceleration as she records these on the whiteboard. "Remember," she explains as she writes, "speed equals the total distance divided by the total time. Acceleration equals the final velocity minus average velocity divided by total time." She finishes writing, asks for questions, and quickly directs the students back to their tasks of testing, recording, discussing, and figuring.

> The atmosphere of Ms. Berge's classroom is simultaneously relaxed, frenetic, and intellectually focused.

The atmosphere of Ms. Berge's classroom is simultaneously relaxed, frenetic, and intellectually focused. The students have much freedom to move around as they work on the lab task. Ms. Berge walks calmly among them, checking progress and assisting as hands are raised. "So if it's slowing down, it'll go into negative. Right? Think of it as negative acceleration. Speed slowing down," she explains. "We're not talking about a race car, are we? We're talking in centimeters." To another team she reminds, "So always divide by the time of the interval." In most instances, Ms. Berge asks the eighth graders leading or related questions rather than giving them answers: "Now which direction was it going? So what's the acceleration from the start to interval one?"

For a second time during the lab activity, Ms. Berge asks the class to stop and give attention to the front whiteboard. "I'm getting a lot of questions about average velocity. This is similar to average speed," she begins, and turns her head to look at a girl who continues to talk. On the board, Ms. Berge sets up a graph, its vertical axis for speed in centimeters and the horizontal axis for time intervals. She continues with her explanation, helping the students to distinguish average velocity and final velocity.

As the class period draws to a close, Ms. Berge alerts the students, "Two more minutes, then start to clean up." The eighth graders have the option of putting their work in the class's designated hanging file or keeping it in their notebooks. Ms. Berge calls out the names of two girls and asks them to "Please wait outside for a minute." The students exit into the hallway and in a few seconds Ms. Berge follows. Inside the classroom, the students begin to return materials to the green trays, snap papers into notebooks, and pack up their materials for class change.

A teacher of three years, Ms. Berge holds a bachelor of science in biology from the College of New Jersey and a master of teaching in 6–12 science from the nearby University of North Carolina at Chapel Hill. Before coming to McDougle Middle School, Ms. Berge worked three years as a laboratory biologist. She attributes this strong content preparation to her ability to help the young adolescents make connections, though she readily admits that there is a big difference between "knowing it and knowing how to teach it!" She believes in getting students' attention and engaging them quickly. "Usually the classroom activities keep students on task," she assesses. Her multiple sections of science are heterogeneously grouped and comprised of young adolescents with a range of ability levels.

> She tries to handle inappropriate actions "on the spot, without giving them an audience."

"I don't feel like I'm a disciplinarian," Ms. Berge responds, when asked about her classroom management style. "I am not controlling, but I expect respect while others are talking." In the event that disciplinary action needs to take place, Ms. Berge will pull the students aside and talk with them one-on-one. She believes that issues should be kept between teacher and student, and she tries to handle inappropriate actions "on the spot, without giving them an audience." Sometimes lunch detention (e.g., cleaning off tables) works well, according to Ms. Berge. She indicates that she generally doesn't e-mail parents unless a behavior is more drastic, such as cheating. At McDougle Middle School teachers are expected to handle small problems, she explains, and adds with a grin, "Besides, writing referrals is just another thing to do!"

The décor of Ms. Berge's spacious science classroom is simple. The daily agenda and homework assignment are written under the date on the whiteboard in the front. Ms. Berge's desk sits in the center behind by the overhead projector cart and a demonstration table with pull-down mirror. Beside the whiteboard is an informational bulletin board with the caption "Pick Your Knows Bulletin." A message on another front poster by A. Dumbledore of the popular *Harry Potter and the Sorcerer's Stone* (Rowling, 1997) communicates that good choices, more so than our abilities, reflects who we are.

The eighth graders sit at green tables arranged in squares in the center area of the long room. These are angled to face the whiteboard. Hanging files for the different sections of eighth grade science Ms. Berge teaches are just inside the door beside a small storage closet for equipment and supplies. Windows, opening onto a green lawn, run the length of the far left wall. Along another side wall and back are two large sinks and top cabinets for additional storage. Student-made paper globes are suspended on string from the ceiling, and an empty aquarium sits on one of the back counters.

> If they see your shoulder next to theirs, they're encouraged. You then have to push them. Then you go away.

In her brief experience in the classroom, Ms. Berge has already noticed a difference in her young adolescents' self-efficacy about learning science. She comments, "If they see your shoulder next to theirs, they're encouraged. You then have to push them. Then you go away." Ms. Berge explains that teachers have to "go with what the kid is and try to build a relationship," yet she cautions about keeping the line firm between being the students' friend and being their teacher. She believes that teachers who want their students to think they're cool risk losing this distinction. According to Ms. Berge, "That's the downfall."

Ms. Berge's ability to interact personally with her eighth graders and still maintain a professional distance is evident during another class session later in the fall. On this morning in mid-November, the students are seated around the green tables in groups of five or six. Judging by their faces, they are in serious discussion over lab experiments. On the board is written directions from the previous day:

1. Gather notes on your section.

    a. Use a frame to condense notes.
    b. For every main idea, provide an example from either your book or one of your own.
    c. When your section is complete, ask for a transparency to write.

2. Teach your section to the class using your examples to illustrate the meaning.

Scaffolding for Success

Ms. Berge's students use a graphic organizer, referred to as a frame, to structure the essential ideas related to scientific concepts from their textbook readings, a strategy she learned during her teacher preparation at UNC-CH

Figure 6.2 The Organizing Frame

Key Topic is about . . .		
Main Idea	*Main Idea*	*Main Idea*
Buoyancy	Floating and Sinking	Density
Essential Details	*Essential Details*	*Essential Details*
1.	1.	1.
2.	2.	2.
3.	3.	3.

So what? Why is it important to understand this?

SOURCE: Adapted from *The Framing Routine by* Edwin Ellis, Edge Enterprises, Lawrence, Kansas, www.GraphicOrganizers.com.

(see Figure 6.2). For the current task, she had grouped the eighth graders into "specialist teams," each responsible for teaching the class and demonstrating with a lab experiment the concepts in an assigned chapter section. In preparation for the presentations, the students had to collaboratively compact their individual notes using another frame and then record key information on a sheet of acetate to use as a guide for teaching. They also needed to practice the appropriate lab.

Each specialist group has been given a laminated sheet that describes the lab experiments that they will demonstrate for the class. These include The Atomizer, Buoyancy, Density, Bernoulli's Principle, Pressure and Depth, Pressure, and Can You Blow Up a Balloon in a Bottle? (see Figure 6.3). Ms. Berge

Figure 6.3 Physics Lab Experiment Sheet

Can You Blow Up a Balloon in a Bottle?

Purpose

This experiment will illustrate how forces cause pressure in a fluid (air).

Materials

Small balloon
Plastic bottle
Straw

Hypothesis

Ask students to form a hypothesis as to whether or not they can blow up a balloon inside of the bottle. Why or why not?

Procedure

1. Holding the neck of a balloon, insert it into an empty bottle. Make sure that the mouth of the balloon is outside the bottle.
2. Ask for a volunteer to come up and try to inflate the balloon.
3. Now have the volunteer try again, but this time have him or her insert a straw into the bottle next to the balloon.
4. Keep one end of the straw sticking out of the bottle.

Results

In Steps 1 and 2, the volunteer will try and try, but the balloon will only inflate until it seals the neck of the bottle.
In Step 3, the balloon will continue to inflate easily.

Conclusion

Have students explain why the balloon inflated only when the straw was inserted into the bottle.

Blowing up the balloon (force) compressed (pressure) the air trapped inside the bottle, making it difficult to blow the balloon up any further. Inserting the straw allowed the air being compressed inside the bottle to escape.

SOURCE: Used with permission from P. Berge, McDougle Middle School, Chapel Hill, NC, in *Managing the Adolescent Classroom: Lessons From Outstanding Teachers*, by Glenda Beamon Crawford. (2004). Corwin Press, Thousand Oaks, CA. www.corwinpress.com.

informs the teams that she will deliver the transparencies when they indicate they are ready. "You guys are the scuba divers, right?" she asks one group of boys who are dipping a straw into water. Three other students at the back of the room are leaning over a filled sink, blowing into the water. Ms. Berge asks another student, "Are you getting your notes done?"

Ms. Berge continues to monitor as the eighth graders prepare the summary transparencies for their presentations: "Three more minutes. One more minute. Begin cleaning up." She instructs the first team to come to the front overhead and to talk slowly and clearly, referring to their written notes. She instructs the members of the class to use their frames to fill in information about the key concepts. Following the oral delivery, the specialists would demonstrate the experiment. As the students approach the front of the room, Ms. Berge smiles and announces, "I'm done teaching. My job's over." She looks around and says, "Excuse me. You have to be in your seats ready to take notes."

The first presentation proceeds according to Ms. Berge's directions. The students take turns explaining the concepts, formulas, and essential details of their chapter sections. Ms. Berge interjects to clear up some confusion between Newton and Pascal and hands one of the students a marker to make the correction on the transparency. She asks, "Is that why air pressure is from all directions?" One of the presenters responds affirmatively. When it is time to demonstrate the related experiment, Can You Blow Up a Balloon in a Bottle? one of the team members announces the title and asks for a volunteer from the audience. Ms. Berge lowers the reflection mirror over the demonstration table.

High Academic Accountability

One of the student specialists indicates to the class, "I'll read the procedures. The hypothesis you form is whether you think he can blow up the balloon in the bottle or not." He begins to read, "Holding the neck of the balloon . . . " The volunteer student tries to inflate the balloon but to no avail. Amid class laughter, the presenter teases, "Are you a smoker? Why can't you blow up that balloon?" Once the straw is inside the bottle, however, the attempt to blow up the balloon is successful. "Why?" directs the presenter to the audience. Not satisfied with the response someone gives, he probes for a different one. "Yes, because air goes through the straw," he explains. Ms. Berge interjects a question, "So what happens to the pressure when the straw is put in?" The student answers, "It gets lower." Ms. Berge continues, "It equalizes, just like Michael said."

There is only time for one presentation before class change. Ms. Berge gives directions about homework for the next day. She will be attending a workshop; thus a substitute will be in charge. She instructs the class to put their work into their hanging files so it won't get misplaced before her return.

As a relatively new teacher, Ms. Berge feels keenly the challenge of facilitating the learning of multiple sections of thirteen-year-old adolescents. She is modest in her admission that she has much to learn about the strategies of classroom management, though she is honest in her desire to observe in the classrooms of other more experienced teachers. Her advice about classroom management at the middle level is nevertheless sound and realistic: "There is no one answer." With a quick grin Ms. Berge continues, "Besides, I'm still trying to figure out what works for me!"

There is no one answer.

QUESTIONS FOR CONSIDERATION AND RESPONSE

1. How might the personal management styles of Ms. Covington and Ms. Berge be compared and contrasted? How can each approach be developmentally responsive for young adolescents?

Ms. Covington manages by a <u>carefully orchestrated flow of classroom activity.</u> She visually guides new students along the physical perimeter of the life skills classroom, much like Ms. Morris, and sets clear expectations for the use of centers and equipment. She motivates students through <u>choice, self-management,</u> and <u>relevance</u> to personal lives. Movement is allowed and hands-on learning provided, yet the flow of activity is orderly and predictable. Ms. Covington responds to raised hands, rotates systematically among centers, and <u>maintains classroom presence</u> with a calm and expectant demeanor.

Student movement and interaction in Ms. Berge's classroom, though purposeful and academically focused, are more casual. Eighth graders pore over tables, sprawl out on the floor, and spill into the hallway. Ms. Berge moves around and among the clusters of students, checking, probing, and assisting. She's comfortable with the noise level of their discussion and their selected mode of physical interaction. Ms. Berge manages through <u>high expectancy for content mastery, experimentation, and cognitive challenge.</u> The students' <u>accountability</u> lies in the end product of lab analysis and synthesis, mathematical calculation, and group presentation.

The contrast in formality of the two classrooms might be attributed to physical setting, and is reflective of the teachers' individualities and personal preferences. Each teacher's management style, nevertheless, is effective for young adolescents developmentally. Each approach allows <u>movement</u> and social <u>interaction,</u> and each teacher holds students <u>accountable</u> for production or performance. Students learn actively and behave responsibly, and each teacher is comfortable within their respective classroom environments.

Reader's Response: How can I use these ideas in my own teaching?

(Continued)

(Continued)

2. How would you characterize Ms. Berge's approach to engendering responsibility and accountability in the eighth grade science students?	
Ms. Berge's goals for student learning are chiefly academic. Her instructional approach reflects the desire to help the eighth graders gain an understanding of content and acquire the skills for complex calculation, collaborative problem solving, and higher-order thinking. To accomplish this end, Ms. Berge allows the students much latitude. The students have a task for which they know they are ultimately accountable, and they have the <u>directions, materials, assistance, technological tools, and graphics organizers to structure the process.</u> How they reach the task's completion or prepare for a presentation, however, is relatively open-ended. Ms. Berge facilitates and guides the students during the progression, but her role at its completion becomes more formalized. The eighth graders are expected to justify their findings (written lab report) or to put them to the true test of peer review. Ms. Berge becomes the <u>critical assessor of their knowledge accuracy and reasoning acuity.</u> For the eighth graders, this responsibility/accountability model is powerful in its real-life preparation for collaborative problem solving and self-directed initiative. Developmentally, the students should be better prepared intellectually and strategically for the discipline-based learning of high school and college.	*Reader's Response:* How can I use these ideas in my own teaching?
3. With reference to the previous case studies, how do the teachers' differing personalities and preferences impact their classroom management styles?	
The teachers in the preceding case studies seem to know what classroom management approaches work best for them personally and operate accordingly. Their <u>commonalities as responsive to young adolescent learning and development</u> have and will	*Reader's Response:* How can I use these ideas in my own teaching?

(Continued)

continue to be discussed; yet the teachers' unique personalities, talents, and individual inclination shape and enhance their mode of operation. The incorporation of humor, theatrics, storytelling, musical performance, color, artistry, and other forms of <u>personal expression or preference individualize</u> the teachers' classroom management styles and help endear them to their students.

For a more extended and specific response to this question, check the section Knowing What Works for You in Chapter 9.

QUESTION FOR THOUGHT

1. What do you consider to be your personal strengths and preferences? How might they factor into your own classroom management style?

7

Believing Less Is More and Positive Is Better

Simplicity and the power of the positive are the dominant messages in the three case studies that shape Chapter 7. Whether in sixth grade health education class or ninth grade English literature, these teachers work intentionally to create a student-centered classroom where young adolescents feel a personal sense of belonging. Emphasis in each scenario is placed on adolescents' positive emotional and social development as the frame of reference for actions, thinking, and lifestyle.

Case Study 12, Battle of the Sexes, introduces Erica Collis. Though her teaching experience spans only two-and-one-half years, she coordinates the rotation drills of more than 100 students in the McDougle Middle School gymnasium in Chapel Hill, North Carolina, with the skill of a veteran. A health and physical education teacher for Grades 6 through 8, Ms. Collis uses humor, friendly competition, and candor to create a learning atmosphere where students enjoy themselves too much to consider misbehaving.

The seventh grade team of Jennifer Haney and Heather Bowes in Case Study 13 operates on the five Ps of behavior: prepared, prompt, polite, positive, and policies. From the first day and continually throughout the year, these young teachers work to build a high level of respect among their students. Their diligence pays off within the team rooms and in their reputation throughout Hawfields Middle School in Mebane, North Carolina.

Case Study 14, They Call Her "Miss D," opens the door into the ninth grade English literature class of Heather DiLorenzo, a "no tolerance zone" for verbal putdowns. A popular young teacher at Eastern Guilford High School in Greensboro, North Carolina, Ms. DiLorenzo maintains an atmosphere of rigorous academic engagement and nonnegotiable mutual respect.

BATTLE OF THE SEXES

Case Study 12

The sixth graders seem literally to burst through the door of Ms. Collis's mobile unit classroom at the back of the McDougle Middle School property. Jam music blares from the CD player as the twenty-three excited eleven-year-olds take their seats, girls to the left, boys to the right. In the brief time between classes, Ms. Collis has shoved the smaller green tables together to form two large ones. A couple of the boys gyrate to the beat. "They're pumped up," grins Ms. Collis. Today, to culminate the unit, the female students will match wits with their male counterparts on their knowledge of sex education. The long-awaited Battle of the Sexes is about to begin.

"Let's get ready to RUMBLE!!!!!!" Ms. Collis literally yells, as she lays a small stack of handouts on each table. "You know the rules. Points will be taken away if you talk or blurt out answers. We'll go around the table. You'll have fifteen seconds to answer. Stop. Think. Relax. Then look at your handout." The girls guess the number closest to Ms. Collis's choice and the contest begins with "If a sex chromosome has an XY combination, will the baby be a boy or girl?" The first of the girls answers correctly, "Boy," and her teammates clap. Ms. Collis records the point on the whiteboard and directs the next question to the first boy: "The testes are contained in the _____, a layer of smooth skin . . ." She smiles as she corrects his mispronunciation of the right answer and awards the boys' table its first point.

Motivation Through Friendly Competition

The questioning continues at a rapid rate as Ms. Collis moves from student to student, alternating between the two tables: "What is the female reproduction cell?" "What is the term for the release of semen?" When one boy can't answer the question, What is the time when the ovaries shrink and stop releasing eggs? Ms. Collis redirects it to the girls and gets a correct response. More claps. The question, What is the term for the mixture of bodily fluid and sperm? brings some silent giggles from the boys' side.

Ms. Collis is quick to praise during the game. "I like how you're thinking. You're not having to look at your handouts." At one point, Ms. Collis makes a scoring mistake, which is promptly pointed out by the boys. "Oh my," she replies, "I predict I'll make two more of these today!" The question, What is the organ that serves as a barrier separating the baby and the mother's blood while still allowing for nutrients and oxygen? stumps both sides. Ms. Collis explains the answer and refers them all to the handout.

The game proceeds as Ms. Collis moves into bonus. The boys miss again and the girls take a notable lead. One boy protests that he can't find an answer on the handout because it's "cut off!" Quickly checking over his shoulder,

Ms. Collis disagrees and sends the missed question about "kinds of twins who share common . . ." to the girls. "Guys, don't get discouraged. We'll still have a bonus round . . . worth two points!" she offers, in an attempt to cheer them up. When the grumbling continues, Ms. Collis adds firmly, "Gentlemen, if you continue that, you'll lose points that, believe me, you don't need to lose!" The boys shush each other.

The super round of two-point bonuses arrives. The boys gain somewhat, but the girls remain in the lead, even when Ms. Collis throws in a three-pointer. Admitting that she would love to see a tie, she tries once more: "Since the girls started off, I'll give the boys one more question. Then you'll have the same number of start-off questions. Does everybody see that?" One boy asks, "How many points?" "You must focus on the question, grasshopper," she replies, and the students laugh. The game ends with the girls victorious.

Ms. Collis consoles the boys that they played a good game, especially with three of them absent. As the sixth graders leave, Ms. Collis reminds the girls to be "gracious and kind" in their win. The next day, Healthy Food Friday, is planned to mark the last day of the elective. Ms. Collis has a collection of recipes with "healthy substitutions"—apple sauce in brownies instead of oil, for example—and the students have signed up to bring in a nutritious choice.

As a Division I athlete at the University of Kansas, Erica Collis excelled as a high jump star in track and field. She enjoyed the movement and fitness aspect but "hated" the competition. A little friendly competition is fun, though, "especially if the scores can be almost even," she laughs. Her Battle of the Sexes is talked about with anticipation by all of the McDougle sixth graders who take the health elective, and the game is long remembered by former ones. Ms. Collis admits that she always tries to rig the game for a tie, adding, "The students know it. But it never works!" She feels fortunate that the families of her students, many of whom live in the university town of Chapel Hill, value education, including health and physical education. The exuberant Ms. Collis teaches multiple forty-five-minute sections a day of these electives in Grades 6, 7, and 8.

Ms. Collis's brief experience as a substitute at the elementary and high school levels has given her a point of comparison: "Young adolescents are different." They still have "the sweetness and eagerness to please not always found in high school," she explains, "but you must be more authoritative and in tune with them as individual people than with elementary students." She observes that young adolescents "have a lot of pride and it is easily bruised. Once that happens, you have created an enemy, rather than an ally, in learning." She says that she's

> Young adolescents have a lot of pride and it is easily bruised. Once that happens, you have created an enemy, rather than an ally, in learning.

strict, but that she "comes down harshly on *actions*, not the person." Ms. Collis stresses that she respects her students in the same way she would herself like to be respected.

How does Ms. Collis manage the changing sections of electives and more than 100 youngsters in a gymnasium at one time? She reveals that she comes out the first day "hard but fun." Referring to her classroom management style as "preventative and positive," she informs that she immediately "sets her expectations as a teacher and as a human being." She believes that "laying the ground rules down early leaves little room for misunderstandings of my expectations." She's quick to joke and laugh, but she will not tolerate any form of disrespect to her or anyone else in the class. When a problem does arise, she indicates that she tries to deal with it without raising her voice, without calling the office ("It shows you can handle your own problems"), and with a "tight-lipped smile."

Key to Ms. Collis's management finesse is her intentional attempt to set a positive classroom tone. Her expectations, handwritten on a wall chart, are simple:

1. Follow the teacher's directions.

2. Be respectful to yourself and others.

3. Be safe.

4. No food, drink, or gum in class.

5. Bring a late pass if tardy.

After she goes over these, Ms. Collis leads the new students in a brainstorming session of three aspects of a positive classroom learning environment that would enable these expectations to be met. These are (1) how the teacher should treat students, (2) how students should treat each other, and (3) how students should treat the teacher. Typical student-generated ideas include "respect privacy," "hear people out," "no blurting out," "wait patiently," "follow instructions," "no cursing," and "don't act sassy to the teacher." The class suggestions are written on a "Positive Environment" poster that is hung on the classroom wall for the duration of the elective.

Around the walls of Ms. Collis's small mobile unit are other indicators of this positive classroom climate. A colorful banner runs along the back with the title, "I like that I am . . ." On it the students have written one aspect about themselves that they value, such as a good reader or skateboarder. Around the sides of the room are posters, handmade by Ms. Collis, with various quotations, sayings, and proverbs related to showing respect and positive attitude. "I try to use quotes from a range of genders, races, and cultures," Ms. Collis explains about the wall hangings. "I also

I try to use quotes from a range of genders, races, and cultures.

try to make them tie into things we study in here." The back banner, for instance, was created during a self-image unit. On one hanging are the block letters BALANCE. All the posters have a purpose, including one with the heading, "What should I do when I come into Ms. Collis's class?"

Ms. Collis feels fortunate to be in a school where the students seldom need consequences. Generally, a call to a home will correct any wrongdoing. If something sudden happens, such as a fight, she sends the offending students down to the school time-out room, which is appropriately named Chill Out. Most of the time, Ms. Collis is happy to say, "A verbal reprimand is enough for my kids to get back on track. I remind them that this is not the way we talk/act/treat each other/treat me, and so on, and they usually realize that they are not contributing to our positive environment." Sometimes, if students are being "unsafe or cruel," she sits them out of PE: "Most kids *hate* to miss PE class and that straightens them out for the next day."

> Ms. Collis is furthermore a firm believer in routines, and once set, she follows them conscientiously.

Ms. Collis is furthermore a firm believer in routines, and once set, she follows them conscientiously. Her students know what to expect and what is expected of them. When they enter health class, for example, they know to go to their seats, take out any homework and put it on the desk, and begin writing in their health notebooks on the journal topic that is written on the front whiteboard. She assigns seats to the sixth graders by the random draw of numbered cards as they enter the room the first day of elective. Seventh and eighth graders are allowed to choose their own seats until there is any problem. In physical education, Ms. Collis relies on alphabetical assignment for squad lines. This assigned spot is where the students routinely sit when they come into the gymnasium to do warm-up. This procedure seems to be working well one early morning, the day before Halloween.

It's 8:40 and the seventh graders dressed in shorts and tees trickle into the gymnasium. "My spooky pumpkins, get in your lines," Ms. Collis calls. "Who's my gorgeous goblin? Let's hear it for Ed!" The designated squad leader of the week gives the cue to start the jumping jacks as Ms. Collis takes roll on her clipboard. The fifty-plus girls and boys are lined up in rows in the front quadrant of the gym facing the wall. The leaders in each row count as the jumps total twenty. Arm stretches are followed by sit-ups. "Say yeah," yells Ms. Collis, and the students clap. With the warm-ups completed, she begins her directions: "Today we are going to be doing different things. You'll be on the same team but each time the task will change."

For Task 1, each line of students, positioned in four corners of the gym, is instructed to dribble the basketball with left hands diagonally across the court and shoot at the opposite basket. Each shot made is worth one point, and the first team to score five points wins that round. "When your team gets to five," Ms. Collis instructs, "kneel." With the blow of her whistle, the gymnasium is transformed into a frenzy of bouncing balls and squealing twelve-year-olds. Ms. Collis keeps score on the clipboard. "Now listen for the next task," she announces when all are kneeling. The students are told to dribble again with left hands, but this time, to turn and attempt a backward shot. The first group to get a total of six baskets receives fifteen points. Again with the shrill of the whistle, the activity resumes. Ms. Collis turns on the music. Her tall, slender frame moves along the perimeter of the gymnasium as she watches the scrambling twelve-year-olds.

Pacing, Variety, and Movement

The task swiftly changes again as the students are told to dribble around an orange bowling pin in center court and back, without knocking it down.

Dominant hands can be used. When all members of a group complete the drill, the group is to sit on the gym floor. Ms. Collis takes a minute to adjust the number in a couple of the lines and whistles. The music resumes. She calls out encouragement. For another drill, the students dribble around the center circle and back, a tricky maneuver, since the four lines would have to cross over. She allows the teams ten seconds to choose their line order, suggesting that they might want to put stronger dribblers at the front and back. She adds, "Please be thoughtful of others' feelings. For some, basketball isn't a favorite sport!"

The tasks change a couple more times. When one team questions the score, Ms. Collis accepts a correction. "I'll believe you. It's more important to be honest than to win." As the session time dwindles, she tries her now-familiar attempt to even the scores with a simple drill of five in a row, but to no avail: Three of the boys on Team 1 are having too good a day. The winning team is allowed to go first to the locker room to shower and change for the next class.

Ms. Collis is eager to share several other strategies that she feels help to facilitate a positive classroom atmosphere. One of these is the use of a stop signal for cueing students' attention, which is voted on by each seventh and eighth grade class. The seventh graders in health class, for example, picked a popular cartoon: Ms. Collis says, "Sponge Bob," and the students respond, "Square Pants." One class uses, "Don't get mad . . . Get glad." A cue that Ms. Collis uses for all of the sixth grade health classes is the "CHHHH . . . CHHHH . . ." sound. When the students hear Ms. Collis begin, they know to stop whatever they're doing, physically turn to face her, and finish the chant.

Verbal Cueing

Two other practices that positively impact the tone of the classroom, according to Ms. Collis, are the daily journal prompts and the use of a question box. These techniques work particularly well in preempting a unit that may be somewhat awkward to the young adolescents, such as the one on sex education. Ms. Collis prefaces the study with the journal prompt, "Why can human development be an awkward subject for people your age?" Students write responses in their journals and are allowed to put anonymous questions in the question box for discussion. Ms. Collis attests that these strategies "troubleshoot before something arises," and the class is better able to focus on the learning. Several of Ms. Collis's suggestions for smooth and positive classroom management are summarized in her Top 12 best classroom management tips below.

Ms. Collis's Top 12 Best Classroom Management Tips

1. Have a routine and follow it every day.

2. Have clear expectations of what is acceptable behavior and what is not.

3. Set the tone the first day. Establish the positive atmosphere you want and don't let anyone disturb that flow, even yourself!

4. Use a stop signal to save time and manage group work.

5. Build in talking and collaborative time rather than fight for continuous focus or silence.

6. Make one happy call home per day.

7. Play music whenever you're not lecturing. If there is background noise, students don't feel compelled to create it by talking (exception: during tests).

8. Circulate the room constantly.

9. Have phrases that students know the meaning of (exception, "Remember what it means to be a respectful listener. Show that.").

10. Have a central theme or concept that everything ties into.

11. Have set privileges or rewards that only one class or grade level/subject get to have.

12. Use negative consequences as infrequently as possible.

Ms. Collis admits that she chose to teach young adolescents because "it makes me happy." Being a disciplinarian, however, makes her unhappy. She'd rather "talk it out" than make a "big fuss." Her students respond positively and often linger around her desk at class change. When the large group of seventh graders have cleared out of the gymnasium after the basketball drills, Ms. Collis begins setting up for the next group. A slightly built Asian girl comes in and walks over for a hug. As it turns out, this eleven-year-old, who had recently moved to the area from Korea, has language difficulties and learning disabilities that place her on a second grade academic level. Ms. Collis had worked out a plan with the exceptional children's teacher for the girl to be mainstreamed into seventh grade gym class each day. She had additionally asked one of the popular and thoughtful cheerleaders in the class to be the younger girl's "buddy, because it's more cool than me." Apparently, the plan is going well.

DIVIDE AND CONQUER

Case Study 13

Over the whiteboard in the front of Heather Bowes's classroom are five yellow posters. At the head of each is one of five words: prepared, prompt, polite, positive, and policies. These are the Navigator Team's five Ps of appropriate behavior. Underneath each word is a T diagram with the words "sounds like," "looks like," and "feels like" (see Figure 7.1). Student-generated examples of acceptable actions, words, and symbols follow. Similar posters can also be found in Ms. Haney's classroom, adjacent through the adjoining door. At the beginning of the

Student-generated examples of acceptable actions . . .

Figure 7.1 Understanding the Five Ps

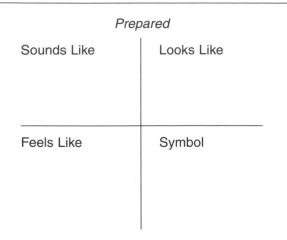

Prepared

Sounds Like	Looks Like
Feels Like	Symbol

school year, the two seventh grade classes meet together as a team to discuss expectations for behavior for the Navigators with regard to the five Ps.

The youthful duo of Bowes and Haney are leaders of a true middle level team. They share approximately sixty seventh graders at Hawfields Middle School in Mebane, North Carolina. Ms. Bowes is responsible for a specialty area of language arts, Ms. Haney handles mathematics, and they team-teach science and social studies on an alternating two-week schedule. Though the two teachers differ in many ways, they share the common team expectation that their students will show respect toward them, each other, and themselves.

Ms. Bowes brought the idea for the five Ps of proper team behavior from her former middle school in another zone of the Alamance-Burlington Schools. The strategy has worked well for the Bowes-Haney team at Hawfields. One example, related to Polite, is the team's polite language policy. The Navigators know that the phrase "Shut up," common in the vernacular of many young adolescents, is a negative line of communication and not acceptable as team talk. The consequence is simple: No talking during lunch. Since young adolescents *live* to talk, especially at lunch, the students make a good effort to avoid using this term, especially after the beginning of the school year. Ms. Haney indicates that the students monitor each other and themselves and know the outcome as soon as they "slip."

The collaborative spirit of the two Navigator teachers goes beyond the setting of common expectations for the team members' behavior. They work together effectively to deal with students individually, and they do so by acknowledging each other's strengths. According to Ms. Haney, "Heather and I work best as a tag team. We are aware of our confrontational weaknesses and limits, and use each other to fill in the needed strengths." Ms. Bowes, for example, is more effective in dealing with the female students, whereas Ms. Haney knows her patience wears thin too quickly with them. The male students, on the other hand, respond better to Ms. Haney and what she refers to as her more "mother form of discipline." Consequently, she often takes the lead in addressing the misbehavior of the boys as the need arises.

Collaborative Teaming

One test of these teachers' ability to negotiate behavior management instinctively came when twelve-year-old T.J. was mainstreamed to the Navigator team from a self-contained block. The boy began the day with Ms. Haney in mathematics, then moved to the science/social studies block, and finished with Ms. Bowes for language arts. While T.J.'s behavior was generally acceptable during the early part of the day, it degenerated into erratic outbursts by the last block. When these disruptions occurred, T.J. was sent to Ms. Haney's side, and he usually calmed down and became productive.

After several weeks, however, T.J. also began to act out for Ms. Haney, and a change was needed. The two teachers quietly worked with the direction of T.J.'s behavioral swings to best benefit him and the others in the class. Although T.J. needed eventually to return to the more structured environment of the self-contained class, the teachers could see some progress in his maturity level and personal behavior. They believe the consistency offered by their concerted efforts helped in some small way, and they felt encouraged when T.J. brought by one of his school pictures one morning.

The complementary differences between the Navigator teachers are apparent in other aspects of their collaborative team management. The extroverted Ms. Bowes loves to set up conferences with parents and discuss the students' progress. According to Ms. Haney, Heather's rapport with parents is "amazing." Mathematician Haney, on the other hand, sees her strength as more analytical, a skill that helps in problem solving. She believes she can generally bring an alternate perspective to an issue or discussion. Their compatibility is evident in their easy interaction with each other and in their mutual enjoyment of their students. Schoolwide, the Bowes-Haney reputation has resulted in other students not on the team showing them the respect that many other teachers are not given.

Although the two Navigator Team teachers work as a unit, they differ further in teaching style and level of personal tolerance for student talking and movement. The physical environment of their respective classrooms is as contrasting as their individual personalities. The following snapshots help to illustrate this divergence.

A check by an item on the sign on Ms. Bowes's classroom door indicates the supplies students will need for the language arts block: literature book; writing, reading, language, and spelling folders; library book; highlighters; pen; and colored pencils. Daily required items are paper, pencil, and planner. Once inside the classroom, the seventh graders follow a morning routine: Unpack book bag and put in cubbies, read overhead to check for supplies needed and collect them, sharpen pencil and fill water bottle, sit in assigned seat, and copy daily agenda in planner.

> I BELIEVE IN YOU. YOU ARE LISTENED TO. I TRUST IN YOU. YOU ARE CARED FOR. YOU ARE VERY IMPORTANT TO ME.

On any given day, a relaxed Ms. Bowes can be seen walking among the students, giving directions, teasing with a few who can't seem to get settled. She might be checking reading logs or planners, speaking in her familiar dramatized voice: "Marvelous! Fabulous! All right!" On a side bulletin board in capital letters is Ms. Bowes's

"Message to My Students": I BELIEVE IN YOU. YOU ARE LISTENED TO. I TRUST IN YOU. YOU ARE CARED FOR. YOU ARE VERY IMPORTANT TO ME. At the front of the room, behind her desk, she has designed another bulletin board that displays a series of pictures from various time periods in her life.

On any given day, the seventh graders themselves might be designing bumper stickers for a European wanting to settle in Africa or, conversely, for the African wanting to be free. They might be reading together from Sean Covey's (1999) *The 7 Habits of Highly Effective Teens*. They might be involved in a discussion of the themes of several young adolescent novels: rewards of persistence, relating to nature, or the power of love. They might be using the criteria on a rubric to grade each other's literature projects: thoughtful, details, originality, accuracy, and effort. ("Never pick a classmate who hates you," Ms. Bowes would cajole.) Or the twelve-year-olds might be making class presentations. One of these presentations had been a two-scene puppet show that illustrated the themes of metamorphosis and death in Taylor's (1969) novel, *The Cay*.

On one day, to introduce the idea of differentiation to the heterogeneously grouped language arts class, Ms. Bowes donned a white lab coat and put sticky notes on several students' desks with the words "Sprained ankle," "Jammed finger," "Cough," and so the ailments went. She then passed out candy "pills" from a paper cup to all the students, saying, "Here's something for your cough. Here's something for your cough. Here's something for your cough." She asked them if a real doctor would use the same remedy for all ailments. They then discussed the need for assignments and different work for different learning needs. Later, when a student complained, "Why does _____ have different work?" or "Why do we have different grades on the same test?" Ms. Bowes simply referred back to the cough medicine remedy-fits-all. She had no more complaints.

Meeting Varying Learning Needs

One of Ms. Bowes's favorite projects is the Person of Eminence Research Project. This semester-long endeavor is described in the following excerpt from a letter she sent to the students' families.

Person of Eminence Research Project

Dear Families,

What an exciting time! We are undergoing a major research project that I feel you should be aware of. We spent this past week in the library researching a person who has made a significant contribution to the world. It has given us an opportunity to find out more about ourselves and the world around us.

What you need to know is that there are in-class and out-of-class portions to this project. The information gathering has taken place the last four days. Students checked out biographies, searched the Internet, and

---

perused encyclopedias. Each month they will have a product to complete. More in-depth instructions will follow. Students are encouraged to continue their quest for knowledge and connection so that the products will be of high quality.

Here is a timeline for the products.

January 8	Scrapbook of life
February 5	Trading Cards
March 5	"Reason for Eminence" Paper
April 2	Birthday Party
May-TBA	Time Warp Tea Party—after school*

* Parents invited, kids dress as person and show off products.

All products will be graded based on the following qualities: neatness, attention to detail, vivid images, wording and insights, as well as accuracy. While typing will help with neatness, it is NOT mandatory. Final products will be accepted in ink if they are not typed.

By the end of this study, your youngster will be an expert on the life of an important person and hopefully make the connection that they too can make an important contribution in the future. Or perhaps they will see how society has grown, just like they have. Nonetheless, it will be exciting to see each part come to fruition.

Please sign and return this letter by Wednesday to show me that you are aware of the magnitude of the project. Feel free to e-mail or call me with any concerns.

Thanks,

Ms. Bowes

Ms. Bowes's management of classroom behavior is as novel as her teaching approach. With so many soccer players in the class, she decided on the idea of yellow cards and red cards. When she holds up a yellow card, the student is verbally warned. The red ones bring the consequences of leaving for the other classroom, documentation in the student's planner, and a call to the parent. According to Ms. Bowes, the seventh graders relate well to the system.

Through the door to the left of Ms. Bowes's desk is a different kind of classroom atmosphere. Prealgebra class is in session, Ms. Haney is standing at the front whiteboard, and homework is being checked. The twenty-four seventh graders are seated at paired desk tables, their attention forward. Ms. Haney briskly writes out the first problem's solution on the board as a girl named Kim calls out the steps. "If you have questions, circle the place and I'll answer in a minute," she directs to the class. The students check their own work, some using red pens, and pass the papers sideways to the end of the rows when the process is completed.

Ms. Haney quickly turns on the overhead projector where she has written on a transparency, "Objective: You will learn to write variable expressions from word phrases and equations from sentences." "Refresh my memory," implores Ms. Haney. "What is an expression?" She then asks a student to define *equation*. "What's the difference?" she probes. "Look at the objective. Where do these expressions come from?" She moves the acetate up so students can copy into their notes: "First choose a variable to represent the unknown number . . ." Ms. Haney refers to a problem: "Eight increased by 5 times a number n, or $8 + 5n$. If you think this is an equation, raise your right hand. If you think it's a phrase, raise your left." She grins, saying that she made it easy for most of them, since they could keep on taking notes. "Josh, you're speaking out of turn," she says as she quickly moves on to the next step. "Can we solve it?"

For another problem, "Six more than twice as many hits," Ms. Haney asks the group, "do I have a variable? What does the phrase tell you?" She cautions them to be careful how the numerical phrase is written: $6 + 2x$ versus $2x + 6$. The lesson continues with a discussion of word and operation relationships. Ms. Haney elicits alternate words for the standard operations of addition, subtraction, multiplication, and division. One student offers "Increased by" for addition. "What else?" Ms. Haney asks. Another student ventures, "Inflate," to which she grins and replies, "You may see it but it might not be that common." A final problem is offered: "The sum of 4 times a number r and 2." With the correct answer given, Ms. Haney again grins, "Hey, I like that!"

The schedule for school health screening interrupts the end of the block. "No homework," Ms. Haney informs. "Five questions on the warm-up will be related to this tomorrow." Ms. Bowes comes in and the two confer about how to recoup the class time that will be missed for the health screening.

The Navigator teachers admit that the student behavior on the team is not always perfect, but that the infractions have more to do with talking or sneaking in gum than ones involving anger or bad attitude. Ms. Haney cites an example during seventh grade lunch to support this assessment. Twice in the previous week the lunchroom had been the scene of disruptive behaviors on other teams: food being spilled, loud booing, and the start of a fight. In each instance, the teachers had to calm down the students and deal with the unruly individuals. "Our students," Ms. Haney relates, "looked for our reaction, letting us know they were not part of the poor behavior." The Navigator Team's expressions, however, didn't convey fear of the teachers or the consequences but rather, according to Ms. Haney, more of an "Oh my gosh, can you believe they are acting like that" attitude.

Meeting the needs of and motivating the range of seventh grade learners on the Navigator Team is a continual challenge. Approximately one-third is academically and intellectually gifted, more than half are not on grade level, and racial diversity is high. All of the students, nevertheless, are held accountable on the end-of-grade (EOG) assessments. For prealgebra, the young adolescents study the same topics. "I just have to start at different levels," Ms. Haney indicates. With the range of reading levels, Ms. Bowes tries to differentiate with shorter tasks and different ways of teaching the literary elements the students are expected to know and understand. The theme of metamorphosis might be best illustrated through Dr. Seuss's (Geisel, 1957) classic, *How the Grinch Stole Christmas*, for example. The two teachers have also divided the students by gender for one of the two-week science units.

> With the range of reading levels, Ms. Bowes tries to differentiate with shorter tasks and different ways of teaching the literary elements the students are expected to know and understand.

At one point in the semester, when Ms. Bowes felt she wasn't motivating some of the African American boys on the team, she had the class read Jerry Spinelli's (1997) novel *Crash* and to create a guide for the main character on the do's and don'ts of winning a teenage girl's heart. The task was an immediate hit, and she felt she was able to make a connection. "It's about giving an opportunity for success," Ms. Bowes ventures. "I guess they didn't believe in themselves earlier. Besides, you catch more bees with honey than with vinegar."

The team of Bowes and Haney acknowledge the strength of their differences as well as the fortitude of their common philosophy: They choose to provide support rather than confrontation. "Education is a hard business," admits Ms. Bowes. "You can't see how much you've sold or earned. We try to look far ahead in their lives and focus on positive attitudes and actions." These teachers share strong pride in the young adolescents on the Navigator Team: "It took them buying into our plan to see how it benefits them, to make it work," Ms. Haney summarizes. "We can see a real change in their attitudes toward learning. They're more willing to take risks." Ms. Bowes continues, "We are a part of them. We *choose* to sit with them at lunch, even as a silent lunch support group! They enjoy it. It's all in how we treat them." She confesses with a quick smile, "When they're absent, I really miss them."

> It's all in how we treat them.

THEY CALL HER "MISS D"

Case Study 14

The prompt on the front whiteboard explains the somber atmosphere of the ninth grade English literature classroom: "How does it make you feel when you hear that someone close to your age has died? Does it change your reaction when the death is the result of something sudden?"

Students of varying size and dress pore over writing journals, putting their feelings into words on the paper. One girl sits partially secluded by a screen, a lop-eared stuffed animal clutched under one arm. This option is open to any student having a particularly bad day, no questions asked. Just days before, a fatal car accident had claimed the life of an older student in the school community. The perplexing reality of the incident had been impossible to avoid, and Ms. DiLorenzo figured that writing about their feelings could help the fourteen-year-olds sort through the confusion.

The Personal Side of Learning

Heather DiLorenzo has taught English literature at Eastern Guilford High School in the Guilford County Schools since her graduation from nearby Elon University seven years previously. An English major with secondary (9–12) licensure and a former North Carolina Teaching Fellow, she has also taught drama and creative writing, and coached girls' soccer. Miss D. as students call her, manages her classroom around the principles of the three Rs:

Respect . . . Yourself.

Responsibility . . . For your actions.

Reality . . . Life is not a dress rehearsal. Do the right thing the first time because you may not get a second chance.

As evident in the opening scenario, she helps her ninth graders with this last R.

Entering the physical environment of Ms. DiLorenzo's classroom is an experience in itself. Over the whiteboard at the front, a large banner-shaped canopy displays the word "ATHENAEUM" in bold capital letters. A poster picturing the Leaning Tower of Pisa to the right bears the caption "Plan Ahead," and this message is signed by Ms. DiLorenzo: "Unfortunately your careless mistakes will not become international tourist attractions." A diagonal line slashed across a large circle with the word "EXCUSES" sends a related message. Another poster nearby indicates "15 Ways to Be Miserable," including always be serious, always live in the past, blame everyone for your unhappiness, help others but don't allow others to help you, and so on. A "Cats at Play" bulletin board to the left of the whiteboard displays the sports statistics of the Eastern Guilford High Wildcats. Written in blue on one corner of the board are two other messages from Ms. DiLorenzo: "*Athletes:* Please try to contain your bags. They are oozing into student seating areas," and "Missing something? Check the lost and found. It's getting out of hand!"

A Personalized Classroom Environment

Lining the back wall of the classroom is an array of slick sports posters: baseball, track, soccer. Each offers a motivational quotation, and most depict female athletes. Other wall posters feature noted women in history, advertise Broadway plays, espouse the wisdom of Albert Einstein, and trace the evolution of baseball jerseys. A scaled model of the Globe Theater sits high on a cabinet on the left side at the back; displayed on construction paper underneath are numerous photographs Ms. DiLorenzo took on location during a stay in London. Tall bookshelves on the other side of the Globe model hold worn-covered literature books and sets of encyclopedias. On the nearby lost-and-found board are thumbtacked several assorted items, including a hoop earring, hair clip, and a glove.

A large bulletin board in the back of the room, with the title "Reach for the Stars," displays the class's independent reading achievement awards. Covering the far wall by the window is a mural painted by a class that had occupied the room before Ms. DiLorenzo began teaching at Eastern Guilford. On it is the word "Peace" brushed boldly in several languages: *Peace, Pax, Paix, Paz, Pace, Shalom, Friede.* Other shelves and cubbies run the perimeter of the room. Two large fans are positioned at the side and corner for added cross-room cooling during the hot months of school opening. Over the telephone on the wall is written in Ms. DiLorenzo's familiar handwriting, "The answer is 'No,' so don't even ask!"

The No Putdown Zone

A couple of other unique physical features of Ms. DiLorenzo's classroom are the No Putdown Zone, which covers the area of a small bulletin board to the left of the whiteboard, and the small red-and-black stop signs positioned strategically on file cabinets and other no-trespassing areas around the room. Ms. DiLorenzo thought of the idea for the No Putdown Zone as a deterrent to the students' too frequent exchange of disrespectful verbal comments (see Figure 7.2). She solicited their input for the display, and the zone was put into effect as a classroom regulation.

Adhered to the floor near Ms. DiLorenzo's desk is one of the small stop signs with the message, "This area is off-limits for students." The students know and respect that the area on and around the desk is Ms. DiLorenzo's personal space. Behind the desk, which is situated at the front side opposite the classroom door, is a cozy area where Ms. DiLorenzo has positioned numerous framed photographs of friends and family. Her chair sits on a round rug in front of the small refrigerator. More photos (she has an online photography business) line the edge of her desk in front of a large calendar. Her lesson plans, to the left, replicate the board agenda. On the corner of the desk is a small bud vase of pink roses from her garden.

The students' desks are purposefully arranged in the center of the room to accommodate an inverted U-shaped path.

The students' desks are purposefully arranged in the center of the room to accommodate an inverted U-shaped path that allows Ms. DiLorenzo to walk among the students as she teaches. It's a chilly Monday morning in February as the first section of fourteen-year-olds enters in typically boisterous style. A boy with blue-tinted spiked hair calls a greeting to Ms. DiLorenzo as he slides into his desk at the back. Ms. DiLorenzo can be seen moving within the U-space, returning papers and indicating pleasure at their good writing. As lingering conversations taper from the class change, the students look toward Ms. DiLorenzo, who has moved to the front of the classroom. "Put everything away in your desk," she instructs. "You will only need a pencil. You have thirty seconds to get into groups of three." She cues at twenty seconds as the students cluster quickly. "OK, you need to be seated right now."

Figure 7.2 The No Putdown Zone

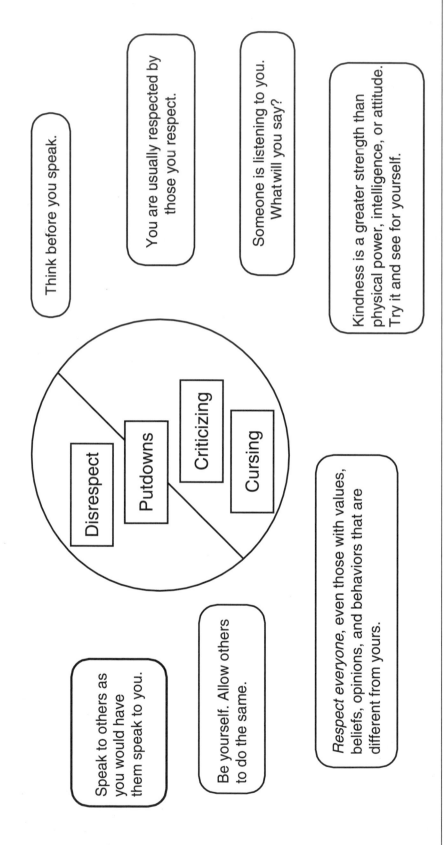

The No Putdown Zone

Think before you speak.

You are usually respected by those you respect.

Someone is listening to you. What will you say?

Kindness is a greater strength than physical power, intelligence, or attitude. Try it and see for yourself.

Disrespect

Putdowns

Criticizing

Cursing

Speak to others as you would have them speak to you.

Be yourself. Allow others to do the same.

Respect everyone, even those with values, beliefs, opinions, and behaviors that are different from yours.

SOURCE: Used with permission from H. DiLorenzo, Eastern Guilford High School, Greensboro, NC, in *Managing the Adolescent Classroom: Lessons From Outstanding Teachers*, by Glenda Beamon Crawford. (2004). Corwin Press, Thousand Oaks, CA. www.corwinpress.com.

On the whiteboard, Ms. DiLorenzo had written a word list that included *setting, protagonist, antagonist, conflict, point of view, tone,* and *mood.* She has also written the following lesson agenda:

1. Insults

2. Shakespeare's language
   a. Skit
   b. Translate
   c. Reenactment

3. Line translations
   a. Group
   b. Independent

4. Prologue—put it all together

To the side of the agenda were written two questions with side messages:

- What makes reading/listening to Shakespeare complicated?
  (You must get past these—to get to these . . .)
- What are the three basic (and I mean basic) topics of Shakespeare's plays?

Ms. DiLorenzo distributes an index card to each student. To each group of three she hands three numbered strips of paper, each containing a different list of insulting words and phrases from Shakespearean plays. She instructs them to divide the lined side of the card into three columns and label each 1, 2, and 3. The students are then directed to take fifteen seconds to choose one word from each list of the three lists and record it on the card in the column with the corresponding number (see Figure 7.3). They are to switch lists until each has a word or phrase in each of the index card columns. This task complete, Ms. DiLorenzo sends the students back to their original desks.

Figure 7.3 Shakespearean Insults

1	2	3
Spleeny	Onion-eyed	Maggot pie

Helping Students to Relate to Content

Quickly handing or tossing Magic Markers, Ms. DiLorenzo instructs the students to write the 1–2–3 words on the other side of the index card large enough to be viewed across the room. She puts an example on the board: "Spleeny onion-eyed maggot pie." She explains that the *new* names would be used instead of their own throughout the period. A boy indicates that his marker is too dry and tosses it back at her hand signal. "Nice catch, Miss D," he calls, and she tosses back another.

During the duration of the lesson, as Ms. DiLorenzo introduces the ninth graders to Shakespeare's unique language and writing style, she refers to them, to their delight, by the new "insult" names. Answering to such names as Infectious Elfskin Bladder, Churlish Flapmouth Lout, and Rank Dog-Hearted Maggot Pie, the students read their way through passages of dialogue. Ms. DiLorenzo helps clarify the meaning of English terminology such as *faire, wherefore, wench, shrew, methinks, betrothed,* and *ere*. At one point, two students agree to dramatize the lines in front of the class—twice! The second time is for more expression, since the meaning of the text should be clearer.

Ms. DiLorenzo continues with mininotes on the differences between blank and rhymed verse and why some of Shakespeare's characters use prose. She reminds the students of the groundlings in the pit of the Globe Theater and inconsequential speech of the commoners of Shakespeare's day. They also discuss why his prevalent themes of sex, violence, and the supernatural were so popular with the people of the period.

Near the end of the briskly paced lesson, the students work individually to identify language styles of six Shakespearean excerpts. Once this activity is checked, Ms. DiLorenzo projects an overhead with three homework questions related to the Prologue:

What style is it written in and why?

What kind of POEM is it?

According to the Prologue, which of the three main topics will be featured in the play?

Ms. DiLorenzo likens the Prologue to a book jacket, and explains that as the play's introduction, it is the first part the audience hears. The class reading of Shakespeare's tragedy *Romeo and Juliet* (1968) begins in two days.

Ms. DiLorenzo describes her classroom management style as "very laid back and interactive." She indicates, "I do not yell at the students, I talk to them. My expectations are clear from Day 1, so they always know what I expect and what *they* can expect from me." She acknowledges that she does not like to talk over students: "I don't. They just stop." She adamantly believes that students should be engaged in learning at all times, and the pacing, variety, and complexity of the Shakespearean introduction are evidence. She admits that keeping up the energy to maintain this level of instructional quality and to manage student behavior consistently are her greatest challenges.

> They need more structure than they are often given.

Ms. DiLorenzo further believes that too much responsibility for personal management is often put on students too soon, especially at fourteen, when they may not be mature enough to do so: "They need more structure than they are often given." She recognizes that adolescents bring with them so many issues that extend beyond the classroom. Accordingly, she sets definite expectations and insists that students follow them. A written copy is handed out and discussed the first day of class.

Ms. DiLorenzo stresses that she keeps these expectations simple and does not allow students to bypass them due to personal wants or reasons. "I treat them as individuals, and I insist that they perform their best. I do not allow much time to stray off course," she adds with a smile. A slender figure sporting a trendy haircut and funky glasses, Ms. DiLorenzo additionally cautions, "You are a more effective leader/facilitator if you avoid trying to be a *buddy*." She cares about her students, but she is diligent about maintaining that balance.

> You are a more effective leader/facilitator if you avoid trying to be a *buddy*.

Ms. DiLorenzo is greatly concerned about how to meet the needs of the students in her classes for whom English is a second language. Besides students who are Hispanic, eight of whom can barely write in their own language, she has one Chinese, two Vietnamese, and several Asian students with differing dialects. She has approached the local university for tutors and sought help through the county adult literacy program. She has also begun teaming with another English teacher at Eastern Guilford who shares a common planning period. While the teachers' pooling of resources, expertise, and teaching strategies has benefited the traditional students, Ms. DiLorenzo has also seen progress with their English-as-a-second-language (ESL) classmates. A set of Hispanic twins, Alicia and José, passed the reading comprehension test. Ms. DiLorenzo cried.

It's still Monday morning, and with the ring of the tardy bell, a new, larger, and livelier group of ninth graders fills Ms. DiLorenzo's chilly classroom. "Excuse me," her voice is heard. "I'm not sure, but I think that was the bell!" She quickly checks roll by shuffling through a stack of small cards, turning any over to record the date for an absence. The intercom comes on for morning announcements, and a boy in the front seat points out that Ms. DiLorenzo has a black marker smudge on her white knit shirt.

Noting that a few students in first period had been confused about which Shakespearean insult words to copy into which column on their index cards (so the noun would be in Column 3!), Ms. DiLorenzo distributes these cards and directs the students to number the three columns before she directs their movement into groups. "We have twenty-four people, so that will give us eight groups of three. You have ten seconds to move." At the precise time, she continues, "Contrary to what you might believe, I didn't put you into groups to talk. Yeah, bummer. I have a task for you." As she gives out the numbered strips of insults, one boy asks, "What's this for?" "You'll find out," Ms. DiLorenzo replies. "Cool," he returns, and second period's introductory lesson on reading and understanding the language of Shakespeare begins.

> She sincerely wants them to know that she is a real person who happens to be their teacher.

Once again, Ms. DiLorenzo iterates the challenge to maintain the student-teacher division and to still play around with them. "They're fun, still kids, and I like to joke and laugh with them." She sincerely wants them to know that she is a real person who happens to be their teacher. "Some days," she admits, "I'd like to just go in and talk."

QUESTIONS FOR CONSIDERATION AND RESPONSE

1. How does Ms. Collis create and maintain a positive environment for young adolescent learning? How are her strengths as a classroom manager and teacher interrelated?

Ms. Collis's strength as classroom manager lies in her ability to create a <u>positive environment</u> where students want to be, feel good about themselves, and treat each other with consideration. She builds this atmosphere intentionally from the first day of the elective by <u>using the students' ideas</u> for behavior in a positive classroom to structure it. Ms. Collis uses creative posters to convey uplifting messages and bulletin boards to support instruction and to display the students' work. Her communication with the young adolescents is open and candid, revealing personal preferences (e.g., about competition). She interjects <u>humor</u>, relates to their youthful culture, and <u>doesn't mind laughing with them and at herself</u>. Whether in the confines of the mobile unit or the space of the gymnasium, she manages behavior and instruction with <u>predictable routine</u>, high <u>time engagement</u>, and <u>varied and fast-paced interaction</u>.

Ms. Collis's classroom management style transfers powerfully into her personal success as a teacher. The students like and respect her, know that their ideas and requests are valued, and rise to the challenge of her questions and instructional tasks. The sixth graders in particular relate well to the <u>supportive and transitional</u> nature of her classroom, where they feel emotionally safe to express and participate. Ms. Collis is also consistent and expectant both behaviorally and academically, and the students respect her and respond positively to her as a teacher. In these many ways, Ms. Collis's classroom management and instructional effectiveness are closely interwoven.

Reader's Response: How can I use these ideas in my own teaching?

(Continued)

(Continued)

2. How do these teachers on the Navigator Team use individual strengths to work together effectively? How do they create a positive learning environment for the seventh graders?

Ms. Haney and Ms. Bowes openly acknowledge their differences yet are resolute in their shared philosophy and goals for the Navigator Team. The environment they strive to establish revolves around the centrality of the five Ps. Like Ms. Collis, they spend time initially with the seventh graders exploring and determining how positive behaviors manifest within the team community. These agreed-upon actions become team practices (with some expectable mishaps early on) throughout the year. The teachers' strengths, personalities, and preferences are different and complementary. Ms. Bowes is theatrical and animated; her physical presence in the classroom is felt by students actively and symbolically (messages, pictures, personal memorabilia). Ms. Haney, on the other hand, admits that her personal style is less flamboyant. Her strengths lie in an ability to translate the complexities of prealgebra into language that is understandable to the young adolescents and their budding capacity for abstract thought. Ms. Haney acknowledges that she is more effective in a setting with less movement and more focused teacher-student interaction.

Collectively, the two teachers have built a team environment that supports young adolescents developmentally. Students have the freedom to experiment, explore, and create through projects and small-group interaction. They are also helped to acquire the intellectual discipline and cognitive skills for higher-level content mathematics. Within this positive, supportive, and expectant team setting, students further gain understanding of appropriate personal behavior. The high regard that the team and students hold within the school is good evidence that these

Reader's Response: How can I use these ideas in my own teaching?

(Continued)

(Continued)

self-management skills transfer beyond the teachers' immediate influence.	
3. How do the affective, cognitive, and physical dimensions of Ms. DiLorenzo's classroom management approach effectively interrelate? In what ways does she convey that she cares about the ninth graders?	
Ms. DiLorenzo's classroom management style combines content rigor, skillful time management, opportunity for social interaction, movement and personal expression, and a no-nonsense expectation for respectful interpersonal communication. She has established an environment enveloped by handwritten messages, motivational posters, personal photographs, and respect for privacy. It is an emotionally safe and relaxed place for the ninth graders to take a needed risk with the complexity of Shakespearean language and its interpretation. Like many of the preceding teachers, Ms. DiLorenzo conscientiously helps the students make connections with academic content by building in relevance (analogies, the insulting name game, vocabulary, humor) and active involvement (small-group collaboration, dramatic reading, discussion, individual response, journaling). She alerts the students for efficient transitions and guides their thinking with questioning and summary. Her meticulous planning, reflected in the board agenda, overheads, prepared materials, and instructional pacing, provides the structure she knows the ninth graders need developmentally. Young adolescents know they are cared about and valued when their ideas are elicited, when they are given <u>multiple opportunities to learn and succeed</u>, and when they know they are surrounded by an environment of respect and goodwill. Ms. DiLorenzo manages with a <u>personal style of caring and expectation</u>, and her students respond.	*Reader's Response:* How can I use these ideas in my own teaching?

8

The School Context

The climate of the school and the philosophy of the administration play a significant role in setting the tone for classroom life. The schools in this book are safe and caring environments where teachers are trusted to make good decisions about instruction, classroom management, and student discipline. School leaders understand the developmental needs of young adolescents and accordingly set high expectations for the academic achievement in individual classrooms. In supportive schools such as these, teachers feel empowered and students are more motivated to engage and to learn (Payne, 2001).

The following sections describe the five school settings related to general geographical locations and schoolwide expectations for classroom and behavioral management. Data sources are questionnaires, observations, and informal meetings with administrators regarding personal and school philosophy.

EASTERN GUILFORD MIDDLE SCHOOL (6–9)

Eastern Guilford Middle School is located in Greensboro, North Carolina, in the eastern end of the large consolidated Guilford County Schools. Approximately five years in its new facility, the middle school is situated on a spacious lot bordered by woods and farmland and is one of the feeder schools for Eastern Guilford High School. The student body is nearly 900, and full-time teaching faculty number at 65. The racial composition of students is 44 percent Caucasian, 42 percent African American, 5 percent Latino, 1 percent Native American, and 13 percent multiracial. The faculty racial makeup is 80 percent Caucasian and 20 percent African American.

My main contact for this book project was with Betty Parrott, the curriculum facilitator, a former middle grades teacher who characterizes her leadership style in the following way: "I provide clear, organized expectations and offer support, information, and skills. I elicit and value collegial input on all decisions and view our school staff as a team and family." Her responses to questions related to classroom management and young adolescent development follow:

What expectations does Eastern Guilford Middle set regarding classroom management?

Each teacher is expected to provide and maintain a stimulating, safe, and positive environment conducive to optimal learning. Student talk and movement should be related to the assigned tasks.

How do you perceive classroom management different for young adolescents (ages ten through fourteen) as compared to lower elementary or high school?

Young adolescents require changes in types of activities and behaviors more often. Successful management of a middle level classroom is dependent upon a clear understanding of adolescent behavior and the ability to pick your battles, focusing on managing those behaviors most important to learning and ignoring the others.

How do you believe Eastern Guilford Middle to be responsive to the unique needs of the young adolescent?

Our school management policy provides students with opportunities to learn from mistakes along with individual behavior plans especially designed for the individual needs of the student.

What advice would you give a novice teacher of young adolescents?

My advice would be to have a management plan that is enforced consistently. But more important, a teacher must genuinely *like* kids in order to be successful.

Teachers in Case Studies: Lisa Wilson (Chapter 3), Barry McDougald (Chapter 4), and Angela Morris (Chapter 5).

EASTERN GUILFORD HIGH SCHOOL (9–12)

Eastern Guilford High School is located on a campus bordering the middle school in Greensboro, North Carolina, in the Guilford County Schools. Dan Cunningham, a principal of seventeen years' experience, is in his second year of head administration at the school. The student body is sized at 963, with 69 full-time teaching faculty. Fifty-four percent of the students are Caucasian, 36 percent are African American, 4 percent are Asian, 4 percent are Latino, and 2 percent are multiracial. As school leader, Mr. Cunningham views his management style as "participatory . . . allowing others to be involved in the decision-making process." He believes that all faculty must be a "part of the larger whole and contribute in a positive manner."

Mr. Cunningham's expectations for classroom management are closely connected with teacher preparation and instructional practice. He believes that students should be on task and performing at the level of interest that keeps them engaged in learning. He also believes that good student interaction and participation in class are critical. He understands that classroom management for the ninth graders in his high school is different and that teachers must meet these students' needs developmentally. He describes young adolescents as more active and more easily distracted than older youth. These students also have varying interests and often cannot see or envision the need to invest time and energy in school. He is clear about the importance of assigning teachers for young adolescents who are creative and use outstanding instructional techniques. He offers the following advice for a novice teacher of young adolescents: "Be prepared and be prepared. Good interaction and good preparation are the key to good classroom management. Also, get in touch with the interests of the students in the classroom."

Teacher in Case Study: Heather DiLorenzo (Chapter 7).

HAWFIELDS MIDDLE SCHOOL (6–8)

In the adjacent Alamance-Burlington System near Mebane, North Carolina, is Hawfields Middle School. Opened in 2000 to accommodate the swell in population in the eastern part of Alamance County, Hawfields shares property and a media center and was modeled after McDougle Middle School in nearby Chapel Hill. Clara Daniels, a twelve-year veteran, is the principal of this school of approximately 650 students and 52 full-time teachers. The largest-growing segment of the student population is Latino.

The first three schoolwide rules at Hawfields are simple and utilitarian: (1) Walk on the right side of the hallway and use doors to the right, (2) choose to chew gum after school hours and outside the building, and (3) abide by system and school expectations. The fourth sets the code of conduct for interaction in the school: "All Huskies will show RESPECT, earn RESPECT, and can expect the RESPECT from others."

Ms. Daniels characterizes her personal management style as flexible and open. She is clear about her view of the interrelatedness of classroom management and the facilitation of student learning. She states, "An environment conducive for learning must be reflected in the management plan." She is also firm in the belief that management of classrooms for adolescents must take into consideration the developmental characteristics of this group. Her leadership at Hawfields Middle guides the school in structuring activities that are developmentally responsive to this age group.

Ms. Daniels's multiple licensure areas, which include elementary education, reading, behaviorally and emotionally handicapped (BEH), social studies, physical education, and curriculum specialist, provide a broad foundation for her understanding of the behavioral and learning needs of young adolescents. Her advice to new middle level teachers is to "be real and know your students." At Hawfields Middle, she knows every student by name and greets them accordingly in the hallway. Her leadership by example sets the tone for Hawfields.

Teachers in Case Studies: Mike Armstrong (Chapter 3), Joyce Covington (Chapter 6), and Heather Bowes and Jennifer Haney (Chapter 7).

McDOUGLE MIDDLE SCHOOL (6–8)

Charley Stewart opened McDougle Middle School in 1994 as its first and only principal. With its student body size of 630 and full-time teaching staff of 60, McDougle is located in the Chapel Hill-Carrboro Schools approximately fifteen miles from the University of North Carolina. McDougle Middle shares property and a media center with the adjacent elementary school. The racial composition of the student body is 74.5 percent Caucasian, 13.4 percent African American, 3.7 percent Asian, 6.2 percent Latino, and 3.2 percent multiracial. Mr. Stewart characterizes his personal leadership style as "laid back and participatory." McDougle Middle School's mission statement can be seen below. Mr. Stewart's responses regarding classroom management expectations and young adolescents follow:

What expectations do you set for McDougle Middle regarding classroom management?

I feel that teachers are best served when they make every effort to handle management issues, with the help of parents, before they ask for administrative assistance. To send a student to the office gives the message that the teacher cannot control the student. I know that there is a range of tolerance levels for noise and movement, and I am comfortable with just about whatever the teachers want as long as it is safe and the students can learn.

How do you perceive classroom management different for young adolescents (ages ten through fourteen) as compared to lower elementary or high school?

There is a great need in the middle grades for students to move, change activities often, and to socialize. If teachers factor these needs into their lesson planning, they have fewer battles to fight.

How do you believe McDougle Middle to be responsive to the unique needs of the young adolescent?

We have a range of resources for individual needs. Teachers are encouraged to differentiate as well as to seek individual help for students who need it.

What advice would you give a novice teacher of young adolescents?

Work on relationships with students and parents, and make sure that the students know you care about them. If behavior starts to break down, look first at your lesson design, second at your class structure, third at your relationship with students and parents, and then think about what needs individual students might have that we are not meeting.

Teachers in Case Studies: Priscilla Dennison (Chapter 2), Patricia Berge (Chapter 6). and Erica Collis (Chapter 7).

McDOUGLE MIDDLE BELIEF STATEMENTS

We believe that for our school to be highly effective, all staff members must share a common philosophy; therefore, we will implement a program based on the following set of beliefs:

1. We believe that all students are capable of high achievement and that intelligence is developed and achievement results from consistent and effective effort; therefore, we will encourage students to meet expectations of excellence.

2. We believe that students learn best when they are actively involved in the learning process; therefore, we will promote active learning and be responsive to student interests and allow students to make choices.

3. We believe that students should develop the capacity to be self-directed learners; therefore, we will teach students to use their time productively, to select challenging activities, and to learn independently.

4. We believe that students need close relationships with adults and peers; therefore, we will meet with students on a regular basis in small groups to address their personal and academic development.

5. We believe that students should be contributing members of both the school and larger communities; therefore, we will nurture a sense of community and individual responsibility for that community.

6. We believe that adolescence is a period of significant physical, social, and emotional change; therefore, we will educate students about those changes in a caring environment that builds self-confidence through self-awareness.

7. We believe that each student is unique; therefore, we will challenge and stimulate all students, recognize and address their individual needs, and help them learn to advocate for their individual needs.

8. We believe that students learn best when they collaborate within diverse groups; therefore, we will group students heterogeneously for instruction in most situations.

9. We believe that students must be prepared for a future of rapid change; therefore, we will foster the abilities to reason, to solve problems, and to use technology as a significant tool for learning.

SOURCE: Used with permission from C. Stewart, McDougle Middle School, Chapel Hill, NC, in *Managing the Adolescent Classroom: Lessons From Outstanding Teachers,* by Glenda Beamon Crawford. (2004). Corwin Press, Thousand Oaks, CA. www.corwinpress.com.

NEW HOPE ELEMENTARY SCHOOL (PRE-K–5)

New Hope Elementary School opened in 1991 in the Orange County Schools in Chapel Hill, North Carolina. Recent redistricting in support of neighborhood schools has shifted the percentage of minority representation (African American, Native American, Asian, and multiracial) downward to 19 percent; however, as many as 30 percent of New Hope's 443 students have low socio-economic status. Barbara Chapman, who joined New Hope as principal in 1997, holds a doctorate in curriculum and instruction from the University of North Carolina at Chapel Hill. The Orange County Schools' Principal of the Year, Dr. Chapman describes herself as a "leader of instructors." She believes that her key role is to make certain New Hope's 36 full-time teachers have the support and services necessary for students to learn well.

Dr. Chapman's classroom management philosophy is based on an understanding of basic human needs, motivation, and effective instructional practice. Feed a child if he or she is hungry, she explains with reference to Maslow's (1998) hierarchy, and then address the inappropriate behavior. All students need to feel a sense of love and belonging, she asserts. They also need to feel they have the power and the capability to make good choices about personal actions. Too often, she explains, teachers rely too heavily on extrinsic rewards, such as superficial praise or tangible tokens, to motivate students to act according to expectations or to achieve academically. When teachers involve students in learning experiences where they have meaningful engagement, students are motivated intrinsically to do the best they can. The derivative of discipline is disciple, she reminds: "It comes from teaching people and helping them to learn how to live life."

What expectations do you set for New Hope Elementary regarding classroom management?

Dr. Chapman believes that instruction should be of such high quality that students are authentically engaged in learning experiences that are worthwhile and satisfying. When this caliber of teaching takes place, students are generally not disrupting class! She is concerned that when misbehavior does occur, too often teachers equate consequences with punishment. Sometimes students just need to be reminded, she ventures, citing the beliefs of current theorists in the field (Gossen, 1996; Kohn, 1996, 1999). She advises her faculty to set up social contracts with students that shift responsibility to students in determining behavioral goals and steps of action. With reference to Gossen's concept of restitution, Dr. Chapman believes in an approach to discipline that helps students make the right choices intrinsically rather than in response to external rewards and punitive consequences.

How do you perceive classroom management different for young adolescents (ages ten through fourteen) as compared to lower elementary or high school?

Having been an assistant principal in a middle school for a number of years before her tenure at New Hope, Dr. Chapman has knowledge of young adolescents and their actions. Successful teachers of adolescents, she contends, understand that behavior is related more to who they are than a personal affront to the teacher. Adolescents don't get up in the morning planning to make a teacher's life miserable, she notes. Trying to control them is like trying to control running water: It will just turn in another direction. The best teachers know that young adolescents need to feel connected and cared about, and they teach with respect for their intellectual capability and need for authentic engagement. Classroom management is thus less a power struggle than finding a way for young adolescents to feel successful, empowered, and personally responsible.

How do you believe New Hope Elementary School to be responsive to the unique needs of the young adolescent?

Dr. Chapman firmly believes that for young adolescents to feel empowered and intrinsically motivated, they need the opportunity to reach out and care about others. She supports and encourages learning experiences, including book buddies, Critter Island, and nature trail leadership, that involve students in "real stuff."

What advice would you give a novice teacher of young adolescents?

Dr. Chapman's fifteen years as an instructional leader and thirty-five years as an educator inform her advice to novice teachers of young adolescents. Accept early, she cautions, that "there is no silver bullet—one way that will work at all times with everyone." She suggests that teachers start with small steps and give themselves permission not to do it all immediately with perfection. Remember that young people need love, care, acceptance, and opportunity for responsibility; they will thrive in a fulfilling place where they have the freedom and expectation to develop a level of independence and purpose.

Teacher in Case Study: John Waszak (Chapter 4).

TURRENTINE MIDDLE SCHOOL (6–8)

Built in the early 1960s as a junior high school, Turrentine Middle School is located in the central part of the Alamance-Burlington Schools. With a teaching faculty of 61, Turrentine Middle School's student population of 1,060 is 59 percent Caucasian, 29 percent African American, 6 percent Latino, 3 percent Asian, and approximately 1 percent multiracial. In his second year as principal, Stephen Gainey characterizes his leadership style in the following way:

> I am a very hands-on administrator. I stay out among the students
> and faculty as much as possible. Furthermore, I feel responsible
> for every facet of the school—thus, I fully educate myself on all aspects
> of the school program, including duties assigned to other members

of my staff. In addition, as principal I feel that I should be involved in ground-level issues on campus such as student discipline. Therefore, I approach my work with my assistant principals and teachers as being a member of one big team.

Dr. Gainey's responses to questions related to classroom management and young adolescent development follow:

What expectations do you set for Turrentine Middle School regarding classroom management?

I expect teachers to manage their classrooms effectively by leading their classes with high-quality instruction. Nonetheless, my teachers are aware that disruptive students will not be allowed to remain in classrooms and deny the delivery of an education to other students.

How do you perceive classroom management different for young adolescents (ages ten through fourteen) as compared to lower elementary or high school?

With classroom management for the ten- through fourteen-year-old, you have to remember their ever-changing moods. Thus, you cannot be quick to judge them as good or bad—because they change dramatically from day to day. As a result, you simply have to take it day by day.

How do you believe Turrentine Middle School to be responsive to the unique needs of the young adolescent?

At Turrentine, our teachers reach out to students in multiple ways such as parent contact, individual student conferences, and the provision of extracurricular activities aimed at their special interests.

What advice would you give a novice teacher of young adolescents?

Don't give up on the students, even if they have bad days or weeks or months in your classroom. Students will rise to your expectations over time, so keep your standards and expectations of them high (no one rises to low expectations). Ignore the bad press adolescents seem to be saddled with these days. Working with this age will be one of your best experiences ever, so hang in there and remember that you will be making a big impact on this country's future through your daily efforts in your classroom.

Teachers in Case Studies: Andrew Fox (Chapter 2), Melaine Rickard (Chapter 3), and Jodi Hofberg (Chapter 5).

The schools, much like the classrooms we visited, are caring places focused on young adolescent learning. Expectations for appropriate student behavior are high, but also clear are expectations the administrators have for academically stimulating and developmentally responsive instructional practice. Common is the belief that motivating teaching and student-centered classrooms are proactive management techniques, and they trust teachers to make good decisions related to any needed disciplinary action. Although the administrators share the belief that the initial action for inappropriate student behavior should be taken at the classroom level, they make their support for teachers known. These administrators are advocates for young adolescents, and their leadership is visible, active, and intentional in creating a safe, positive, and nurturing school environment for student achievement and personal growth.

9

How the Best
Middle Level
Teachers Manage

Adolescence is a "formative period when physical change accelerates, social exploration is tentative, and mental capacity is rapidly unfolding" (Beamon, 1997, p. xii). It is an exhilarating time as sexuality awakens, a teen culture of fad and fashion beckons, and long-anticipated independence entices. It is a liberating time when the emerging capacity to choose a personal course of action and to consider the consequences of decisions simultaneously empowers and awes. It is also a time of awkwardness, self-consciousness, and uncertainty as personal identity is negotiated and shaped.

The challenge for young adolescent students in classrooms lies in the transitional nature of this developmental juncture. Traversing the middle ground between childhood and youth means dealing awkwardly with physical and emotional changes, negotiating within uncertain confidence the new social landscape, and grappling with unanswerable questions about a world no longer perceived as black and white.

In the later edition of their long-standing publication, *Promoting Harmony: Young Adolescent Development and School Practices* (Van Hoose et al., 2001), the authors propose that a successful middle school is one "designed around the unique needs of young adolescents" (p. 2). This same statement can be made with regard to each classroom. In an earlier book (Beamon, 1997), I emphasized the need for middle level teachers to structure learning environments that are challenging enough to motivate, structured enough to convey expectation, and active enough to allow movement, social interaction, and experimentation. I justified this structuring by its congruence with young adolescents' developmental needs:

Young adolescents . . . need to form positive peer relationships and caring relationships with adults who like and respect them. They are generally unsure of themselves, and although they are extremely energetic and thrive on experimentation, they need clear structure to help them become responsible decision makers. Young adolescents tend to be self-conscious and self-critical, yet they need to explore creative and diverse talents and to have their accomplishments recognized by those around them. They also need time to reflect on how others perceive them and to integrate these impressions into their evolving identities. (p. 10)

In his recent publication *Day One and Beyond: Practical Matters for New Middle Level Teachers* (2003), Wormelli contends that most problems related to student behavior and disciplinary issues can be associated with "disconnections between teacher practices and student needs" (p. 34). For classroom management to work well at the middle level, teachers must take into account the developmental nature and related learning needs of their students. Because adolescents push for independence and autonomy, they need opportunities for choice, responsibility, and self-direction. Their tentative confidence is less vulnerable in a climate of acceptance and accomplishment. Intellectually, they need instructional relevance, content complexity, and a high level of engagement. Their social concerns for peer acceptance and conformity bring the additional need to work cooperatively and to contribute meaningfully within a group (Beamon, 2001).

The crucial connection between classroom management practices and young adolescents' developmental needs is unwaveringly supported by other professional research in middle level education. In *Turning Points 2000* (Jackson & Davis, 2000), for example, the authors assert that young adolescents need (a) positive social interaction with adults and peers, (b) structure and clear limits, (c) physical activity, (d) creative expression, (e) competence and achievement, (f) meaningful participation in family, school, and community, and (g) opportunities for self-direction. In classrooms that provide these opportunities, young adolescents are better able to acquire social skills, gain autonomy, define identity, and develop the dispositions for ethical, responsible behavior.

The middle level teachers in the preceding case studies have created classroom environments that are developmentally responsive for young adolescents. Their students are members of a purposeful, organized, interactive, and supportive community, one in which they are held responsible and accountable for their personal actions and learning. Expectations for behavior, movement, and treatment of others and property are apparent, yet there appears to be minimal indication of control, punishment, coercion, or power struggle.

The climate of each classroom is more accurately characterized by a belief that given trust, opportunity, and encouragement, most young adolescents will try to do what is expected and appropriate. This philosophical mind-set is not merely grounded in the teachers' understanding of what adolescents need to learn and self-manage but also in basic psychological theory related to the universal human need for autonomy, relatedness, and competence (Deci & Ryan, 1998). Figure 9.1 provides a visual of the developmental relatedness as supported by the middle level research (Jackson & Davis, 2000).

Figure 9.1 Classroom Management and Young Adolescent Developmental Needs

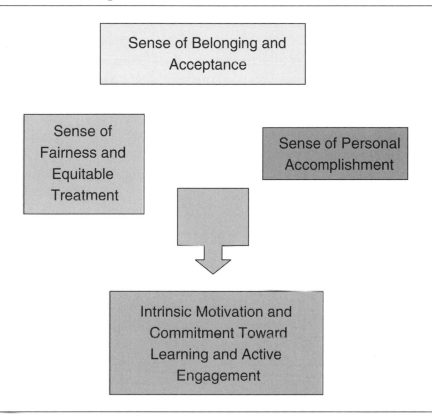

SOURCE: Jackson & Davis (2000).

These middle level teachers do not appear to rely on controlling authority, nor do they seem to have the naive assumption that students will develop personal responsibility magically on their own. Rather, they go shoulder to shoulder with their students, providing a balance of limitation and freedom and helping them to see how their actions impact others. The philosophical belief that human beings are capable of making healthy personal decisions with regard to how they act and treat others is the premise of recent insights into the nature of classroom management (Cummings, 2000; Glasser, 1992; Kohn, 1996, 1999; Marzano, 2003; Wong & Wong, 1998). Kohn (1996) describes this teacher disposition as one guided by the question, What do they require in order to flourish? rather than asking what can be done to get these students to comply (p. 10).

This approach to classroom management additionally resonates with current literature related to brain research. Sylwester (2003), for example, supports a collaborative, community-building classroom environment and contends that "the only way for students to master social and problem-solving skills is to explore and practice them with as much independence as possible" (p. 67). Biologically, he suggests, adolescents are maturing toward the capability for self-managed behavior, but this development is awkward and often characterized by impulsivity. They thus need a classroom where their tentative efforts to acquire the skills for intellectual and social competence are supported. A classroom management system that promotes this development is one that will allow adolescents the freedom to try, fail, reflect on personal actions, and try again without harsh judgment or severe recrimination.

The research questions that prompted the book's underlying research study are explicitly associated with young adolescents' transitional need for independence with limitation, challenge with support, and autonomy within community. These queries encompassed three interrelated dimensions of classroom life:

1. Physical, as related to use of time, procedures, and structural resources

2. Affective, as promoting positive social, emotional, and personal development

3. Cognitive, as defined by intellectual engagement and motivation for learning and self-management

Although these dimensions offer a structure for classifying observed classroom practices, it is important to note that their real impact on adolescent learning and development lies less in their discrete nature and more in the dynamics of their interaction in the classroom environment. Figure 9.2 is an attempt to summarize these observations and to illustrate visually their interconnectedness.

What most powerfully emerged as the research progressed are the six prevalent themes that cut across the varying teacher profiles and helped to shape the chapter organization. It is important to reiterate that while these patterns are more dominant in some of the case studies, each theme can be discerned to some degree in all of them. These patterns of classroom management are supported not only by the research on young adolescent development and learning but also by well-established theories of motivation and self-efficacy. These six themes are discussed with reference to the validating professional literature in the following sections.

MANAGEMENT THROUGH HIGH ENGAGEMENT

As early as John Dewey (1938), educators have recognized the connection between uninspiring instructional practice, student boredom, and impetus to learn. Unfortunately, conclusions drawn in the 1990s by middle level

Figure 9.2   The Interrelated Dimensions of Classroom Management

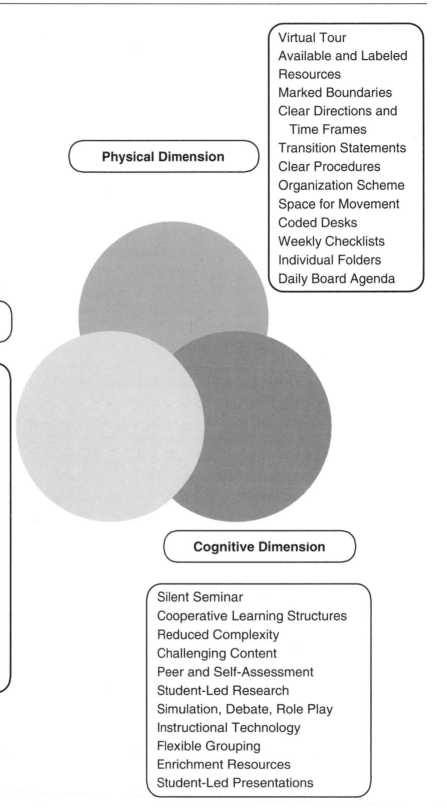

Physical Dimension

Virtual Tour
Available and Labeled
Resources
Marked Boundaries
Clear Directions and
   Time Frames
Transition Statements
Clear Procedures
Organization Scheme
Space for Movement
Coded Desks
Weekly Checklists
Individual Folders
Daily Board Agenda

Affective Dimension

Humor
Friendly Competition
Cooperative Grouping
Journaling
Recognition of Positive
   Behavior
Firm Expectation for
   Appropriate Behavior
Informal Communication
Smiles and Laughter
Fairness and Equitable
   Treatment
Game Format
Positive Reinforcement
Student Choice and Input
Communication of Joy
Mutual Respect

Cognitive Dimension

Silent Seminar
Cooperative Learning Structures
Reduced Complexity
Challenging Content
Peer and Self-Assessment
Student-Led Research
Simulation, Debate, Role Play
Instructional Technology
Flexible Grouping
Enrichment Resources
Student-Led Presentations

researchers report that classrooms continue to be environments of passive learning, drill and practice, and the mindless memorization of facts (Jackson & Davis, 2000). These concerns were part of the impetus to revisit the original recommendations of the 1989 *Turning Points: Preparing American Youth for the 21st Century* (Carnegie Council on Adolescent Development) and to iterate more explicitly the true intent of middle level education:

> Let us be clear. The main purpose of middle grades education is to promote young adolescents' intellectual development. It is to enable every student to think creatively, to identify and solve meaningful problems, to communicate and work well with others, to develop the base of factual knowledge and skills that is the essential foundation for these "higher order" capacities. As they develop these capacities, every young adolescent should be able to meet or exceed high academic standards. (p. 11)

Each middle level teacher profiled in this book provides students with a variety of meaningful and intellectually engaging instruction. Although expectations for student behavior and interaction are clearly communicated, the teachers associate classroom management more with high expectations for academic learning than rules and consequences. A simple test review is transformed into an interactive and motivational experience (Ms. Dennison's "clarify the mush" in Chapter 2 and Ms. Rickard's Jeopardy-style game in Chapter 3). Mr. Fox's students in Chapter 2 participate in a student-led debate that is viewed by other classes and parents and judged by an external figure. Technology facilitates the interaction as Mr. Armstrong's eighth graders conduct high-interest research in Chapter 3, and Ms. Hofberg's sixth graders trade chosen stocks on a simulated market in Chapter 5.

Students in other case studies actively participate in cooperative learning experiences (Ms. Berge's lab teams in Chapter 6, Ms. Rickard's carousel-style silent seminar in Chapter 3, Ms. Wilson's literature circles in Chapter 2, and Mr. Waszak's nature trail teams in Chapter 4). Whether in a battle of the sexes or on the basketball court, Ms. Collis (Chapter 7) keeps her students involved in fast-paced and challenging, yet good-natured, competition. Students in Ms. Covington's classes in Chapter 6 select centers to learn skills that will be important in the future.

In each situation, young adolescents are engaged in motivating learning experiences that involve movement, purposeful interaction, and a high level of instructional time on task. These evidences of management by high engagement are also enhanced by relevance, authenticity, choice, and high interest, criteria important in the learning and motivation of young adolescents (Beamon, 2001; Stevenson, 1998). Current research has linked motivational instruction and academic success with improved student behavior (Rivera & Smith, 1997). Rather than underestimating young adolescents' capability for self-control, middle level teachers fare better by taking a risk with an intellectually engaging strategy, even if it is not the smoothest attempt. In each scenario, the teachers act as facilitators rather than directors, and classroom management takes the form of guidance as students immerse themselves in meaningful learning experiences.

SHIFTING SPEED—NOT LOWERING EXPECTATIONS

Another prevalent belief that permeates the case studies is that all young adolescents should have the opportunity for *appropriately* challenging instruction. Rather than dumbing down the curriculum, these teachers seek ways to reduce the complexity of a task or to simplify an instructional approach without compromising its motivational appeal for students. Ms. Wilson in Chapter 3 modifies a cooperative learning strategy for the Inclusion Block by having the sixth graders focus on one novel rather than several. Mr. Armstrong in the same chapter does not deny Block II the opportunity to explore an area of interest through the I-Search activity, even though he anticipates the need to provide the eighth graders with more assistance and structure in the organization of their papers. "Dr. Bowes" (Chapter 7), with her lab coat and candy pills, teaches the seventh graders a memorable lesson in respecting the different learning needs in the class. With this introduction, she sets the stage for differentiation within the heterogeneous block.

Tomlinson, as cited in *Turning Points 2000* (Jackson & Davis, 2000), offers several characteristics of differentiated classrooms. These include, among others, a focus on what is essential to learn—the important concepts and understandings—rather than isolated facts; ongoing assessment to determine students' readiness, interests, and skills levels; student participation in meaningful, interesting, and appropriately challenging tasks; and a range of instructional strategies that include whole-group, small-group and individual, and teacher and student directed (pp. 78–80). Arnold (2001) advocates that differentiation is a personalized and developmentally appropriate approach because it takes into account young adolescents' needs, interests, and abilities. He recommends gearing instruction to students' individual levels of development and understanding, varying time, pacing, and teaching/learning strategies, teaching a relevant curriculum, and giving students increasing and significant opportunities to assume responsibility (pp. 30–31).

Differentiation in middle level classrooms furthermore involves continual assessment of students' learning needs and flexible modification of the context of instruction. Important to the process, particularly for young adolescents, is their involvement in and awareness of their own learning progress (Beamon, 2001; Jackson & Davis, 2000).

Mr. Fox's management of the instruction in the two heterogeneous blocks in Chapter 2 provides an exemplary example of differentiation in action. His assessment is ongoing, students are involved in the monitoring of their learning progress, and they have the opportunity to move flexibly as essential skills are acquired. Mr. McDougald in Chapter 4 provides a different model. Not lowering expectations for students to learn the elements of literary analysis or grade-level vocabulary, he shifts the context by reading aloud and encouraging student engagement through his board toss and star system. His eighth graders are individually accountable for the homework application; however, he provides a graphic organizer to help them process their thinking.

Other teachers allow flexibility of time (Mr. Armstrong in Chapter 3), choice of assessment or presentation format (Ms. Dennison in Chapter 2 and Ms. Berge in Chapter 6), and opportunity for individual expression (Ms. DiLorenzo's and Ms. Collis's journaling in Chapter 7, Ms. Morris's maze designs in Chapter 5, Mr. Waszak's flexible math solutions in Chapter 4), flexibility of grouping (gender grouping by the team in Chapter 7), and use of self-assessments (Ms. Hofberg's slates in Chapter 5 and Ms. Covington's folder system in Chapter 6). In all cases, genuine effort was made to know their students' needs and to help them be and feel successful. With the right amount of structure, guidance, and assistance, young adolescents can begin to accumulate small successes both academically and behaviorally. These personal victories build confidence and self-efficacy (Bandura, 1993; Beamon, 2001).

Burke (2000) has noted that most disruptions occur when students are either overwhelmed and frustrated or underchallenged and bored; thus this endeavor for the right balance is a continuous one. A critical factor in meeting the needs of a wide range of young adolescent learners lies in helping them to develop the mind-set for personal progress and continuous improvement, however gradual (Beamon, 2001). If young adolescents feel they have some control or power with regard to their learning, they react more positively toward school and are more motivated to invest the personal time and effort to achieve academically. Stevenson (1998), in the second edition of his book *Teaching Ten to Fourteen Year Olds,* summarizes aptly: "When learning is good—that is, meaningful and satisfying to the learner—an individual has opted to commit whatever energy the task requires and make whatever sacrifices the learning necessitates. In short, the learner has chosen to learn" (p. 158).

SHIFTING RESPONSIBILITY TO STUDENTS

Another pervasive pattern throughout the case studies is the expectation for young adolescents to assume responsibility for their learning and personal actions. In my book *Teaching With Adolescent Learning in Mind* (Beamon, 2001), I suggest that young adolescents will begin to take ownership of their learning through the "accumulation of experiences that guide, sometimes nudge, yet consistently and intentionally place responsibility upon the[ir] shoulders" (p. 62). The same notion can be applied to the self-management of behavior. Intellectually, young adolescents are ready. Emerging metacognitive skills enable them to begin to evaluate not only the quality of their academic work but also the impact of their actions on others in the classroom. Accordingly, I wrote,

> Metacognition can afford the intellectual power to assess reactions in situations, to control impulsiveness and temper negative emotions, to think about the consequences of personal decisions, and to act with healthy judgment in social situations. (p. 12)

While young adolescents have the potential to become increasingly self-reflective and self-regulating academically and behaviorally, two other elements must be present in the process: opportunity and guidance. Stevenson

(1998) observes that too often, teachers fail to acknowledge young adolescents' capability to become more accountable for personal actions, decisions, choices, and use of time and thus do not share responsibility with them. Wormelli (2003) suggests that to cultivate these abilities in young adolescents, teachers need to give students "positions of responsibility even when we aren't sure they can handle them" (p. 176). The other consideration for teachers, thus, is in determining the structure and in setting the limitations that help to guide students in their desire to be and be seen as responsible and self-managing human beings. In varying ways and degrees and within specified boundaries, the middle level teachers in the preceding case studies have begun the shift of responsibility to students.

The teacher who most explicitly teaches and manages by a responsibility model is Mr. Waszak, whose classroom is described in Chapter 4. With his honor roll and initial question, Who's responsible for your learning? the fifth graders are offered the choice to assume ownership of personal actions and direction. With success comes privilege in the form of extended opportunity and increased responsibility. Mr. Waszak also realistically does not anticipate perfection and gives his students what Stevenson (1998) refers to as necessary "close but not closed" redemption (p. 225). Mr. Waszak's goal is to prepare his students for the challenges of a middle school where they must act more independently. A related goal is that these ten-year-olds will begin to realize that the locus of control for actions and achievement lies within. For young adolescents, this realization is a powerful one, if indeed attained.

The teachers in the preceding scenarios nurture student responsibility as a classroom management strategy in various ways. Ms. Hofberg's sixth graders in Chapter 5, for example, transition to lockers and lock combinations efficiently. Ms. Morris in the same chapter and Ms. Covington in Chapter 6 place the responsibility for cleanup and classroom maintenance squarely on the shoulders of students. The four teachers in Chapter 7 (Ms. Collis, the Bowes-Haney team, and Ms. DiLorenzo) include students early in the establishment of a code of respect within the learning environment, thus fostering ownership and responsibility for its preservation. Mr. McDougald in Chapter 4 has developed an extraordinary system for classroom administrative management that relies singularly on student assistance.

In each of these situations where student responsibility is an integral part of classroom management, the teachers' limitations, routines, and directions are clearly specified and consistently maintained. Young adolescents sense that they are entrusted to do what is expected and right. Once again, the belief among these teachers is apparent. Human beings, in this case young adolescents, are capable of making healthy personal decisions with regard to how they act, treat others, and respect property.

MAKING THE PHYSICAL ENVIRONMENT A PARTNER

David Perkins (1992) has used the term "person-plus" to describe the purposeful interaction of a student's inner resources with the range of possible supports in the learning environment (p. 132). These supports can be human (the teacher or other students and adults) or assume the symbolic form of graphic organizers (charts, diagrams, concept webs, decision-making structures, flow charts, etc.) or technologies such as computers or graphing calculators. Whatever the external support, student knowledge acquisition and learning are assisted (Beamon, 2001). Prevalent among the middle level teachers is the strategic use of the physical environment as a classroom management technique. I would like to suggest the person-plus theory as a means to explain the effectiveness of this strategy to assist not only the flow of classroom movement and instructional activity but also to facilitate young adolescent learning and personal management.

The decisions a teacher makes about the use of a classroom's physical space are important ones related to movement, interaction, and instructional time-on-task (Cummings, 2000). Preservice teachers have traditionally been required to sketch diagrams of "ideal" classrooms with attention to desk arrangement, group and independent work, "traffic" flow, and placement of centers, equipment, materials, or other physical resources. What appears to be a unique feature in many of the classrooms featured in this book is not the static nature of physical arrangement but in the dynamic use of physical space. The physical environment figuratively emerges as a partner in the management of classroom activity.

The classroom management approaches of the two teachers featured in Chapter 5, Ms. Morris and Ms. Hofberg, and Ms. Covington in Chapter 6 most explicitly illustrate this strategic collaboration with physical surroundings. Necessitated by multiple sections, changing grade levels, and the need for efficient access to supplies and materials, Ms. Morris's art room with its labeled shelves, counters, and cabinets becomes a road map directing movement and instruction. Ms. Hofberg's color-coded environment and lettered desks facilitate a similar flow of activity and organization. For Ms. Covington, the expansive physical environment of work stations, each with explicit directions, seems to assume the persona of a teammate helping in the management of multiple tasks.

Each teacher spends extended time in establishing procedures and in communicating expectations for interaction within the classroom environment; however, when the physical management system is in operation, students assume responsibility for the predictable flow of routine. A teacher's call of a simple direction signals the distribution of materials or the arrangement of groups. By glancing at a designated section of the whiteboard, students know the agenda for the block or period or a homework task. Folders wait in a familiar location and materials are ordered and in ample supply, even with the three to four minutes these teachers have between classes. In all instances, the young adolescents appear to have internalized the plan of activity, and they carry it out in a smooth and fluid manner.

Many of the other middle level teachers also use the physical spaces of classrooms with attention to behavior management, student movement, and instruction. Mr. McDougald in Chapter 4 and Ms. Wilson in Chapter 3 make purposeful use of labeled boxes and work areas. Ms. Collis, Ms. Bowes, Ms. Haney, and Ms. DiLorenzo (Chapter 7) all use posters, charts, bulletin boards, and other physical markers as points of reference for classroom behavior, expectations, and emotional atmosphere.

One side of Mr. Waszak's classroom in Chapter 4 is transformed into a menagerie that assisted him in teaching a hands-on knowledge of science and in promoting student self-esteem, leadership, and responsibility. Ms. Rickard in Chapter 3 uses posters on classroom walls as silent questions to generate thinking and literary response. In all of the classrooms, posters or handwritten messages encourage and motivate, family pictures tell the story of the teachers' personal side, and displays of student work convey an unspoken message that young adolescents are celebrated and valued.

Teachers today face the pressures of time management, vast diversity, and large class size. These teachers deliberately transform what could be a stark place into an inviting, informative, and interactive space for adolescent learning and development. The classroom settings play an integral role in daily routine and instructional activity. Like Perkins's symbolic person-plus learning tools, the physical environment becomes a supportive partner for classroom management and young adolescent intellectual, social, and personal development.

KNOWING WHAT WORKS FOR YOU

In light of the many similarities among the middle level teachers, it is interesting to note their unique differences and distinguishing personal preferences. Emily and I had not expected to find a single style of middle level manager or necessarily a common classroom management technique. We were intrigued nevertheless by the level of confidence and poise each showed in his or her own distinctive approach. These teachers seem to know themselves well—what they like, what they can tolerate, and what they personally *need* to be effective facilitators of young adolescent learning. Even with the range of experience, from two-and-one-half to twenty-seven years, they recognize personal strengths and needs and have established a classroom environment in which they can *themselves* function well. These teachers are furthermore open and candid about their preferences with students. Deiro (1996) identifies appropriate self-disclosure, or "the act of sharing and exposing . . . feelings, attitudes and experiences," as a healthy way to build connections with young adolescents (p. 197).

Mr. McDougald in Chapter 4, for example, admits that he personally finds it difficult to begin class in a timely manner while managing administrative business. Though he acknowledges that this responsibility shift to students is effective in helping the eighth graders feel a sense of importance, the initial impetus was personal. Ms. Collis in Chapter 7 conceded that past experiences have influenced her view of competition, and although physical education is inherently competitive, she downplays it. Her students expect her to do so and they accept it. Ms. Hofberg in Chapter 5 admittedly cannot function in a classroom without ultimate organization, and she has found color to work. In an atmosphere of mutual respect, Ms. DiLorenzo in Chapter 7 uses the strategy of stop signs to take care of her own desire for personal classroom space.

Ms. Dennison in Chapter 2 is candid with her students about her aversion to fragrance and revealing clothing, and they respect her wishes.

Although all the teachers use the physical environment of the classroom advantageously for management purposes, the appearance and use of space within the individual classrooms vary significantly. Ms. Rickard and Ms. Wilson in Chapter 3, and Ms. Bowes in Chapter 7, have created learning environments that might be described as homey. Swag curtains over a window, a wall mirror, tables of seasonal decorations, and a bulletin board of personal pictures from past life events are a few examples of the way these teachers' personalities are reflected in their surroundings. Mr. McDougald's room in Chapter 4 is also colorful and personalized with photographs, plaques, and displays.

Four of the other teachers' classrooms are decorated in a simple, more utilitarian style: Mr. Fox in Chapter 2, Mr. Armstrong in Chapter 3, Ms. Berge in Chapter 6, and Ms. Haney in Chapter 7. Mr. Armstrong, for one, offers no apology for not having an artfully decorated room. "My strength," he indicates, "is more verbal and personally interactive." The varying desk arrangements among the classrooms include clustered small and large tables, long, short, and angled rows, and Ms. DiLorenzo's (Chapter 7) preference of short rows that allow walk space in an inverted U. These differences in the physical appearance of classrooms and in the use of space do not appear to be related to gender, subject area, or years of experience.

Perhaps the most striking variation among the classrooms is the accepted level for student voice volume and freedom of movement. The two teachers in Chapter 6, Ms. Covington and Ms. Berge, are examples of contrasting situations, the first more systematic and orderly, the second less structured and more spontaneous. One could contend that the differences are a product of subject matter and context (physics lab work vs. use of expensive equipment) or the years of experience (three vs. twenty-seven). The variations, however, appear to be more related to what the individuals acknowledge they can and will personally tolerate. In Mr. Armstrong's classroom in Chapter 3, to give another example, students choose their spaces for group work; in Ms. Rickard's room in the same chapter, student movement is carefully guided. Mr. Waszak's fifth graders in Chapter 4 move independently within the class and out; Ms. Morris in Chapter 5 expects the art students to move purposefully within established boundaries within the classroom. The two teachers on the Navigator Team in Chapter 7 recognize personal differences in style and use these advantageously for behavior management and instructional purposes. There is no correct or "right" way; each works for the individual teacher and situation.

Another interesting difference among the middle level teachers is personality and the way their individualities become integral to classroom life. Mr. Fox and Ms. Dennison (Chapter 2) and Ms. Bowes and Ms. Collis (Chapter 7) have a flair for humor and antic, and they use this gift strategically for behavioral management and instructional engagement. Although Ms. Rickard does not affect the Lo-Chow accent of Mr. Fox and exudes a calmer classroom demeanor, she laughs a lot with students and boldly and enthusiastically shows her personal side in tacky green polyester. Mr. Armstrong in Chapter 3 and Mr. McDougald in Chapter 4 gregariously weave personal stories into instruction.

Mr. Waszak in Chapter 4 has a flair for fantasy that is woven into the learning culture of the Land of Woz. Ms. Hofberg and Ms. Morris, both in Chapter 5, manage with friendly yet firm expectations.

Perhaps this pattern of knowing "what works for me" can be attributed to the teachers' own self-esteem that enables them to assert themselves personally and openly to their students. It may be related to the self-efficacy gained through successful experiences in the classroom. These teachers do not try to emulate anyone else, and though all are unassuming, they genuinely believe that their classrooms are good places for young adolescents to learn and develop. They smile frequently, interact freely, and treat students with genial receptiveness. They are not afraid to take a risk with what Wormelli (2003) has referred to as "sharing their humanity" with the young adolescents in order to build the give-and-take relationships needed for the day-to-day management of a productive learning environment (p. 170).

BELIEVING LESS IS MORE AND POSITIVE IS BETTER

Whatever the personality, individual forte, classroom appearance, grade level, or content area, the middle level teachers' expectations for student behavior are consistently simple and positive. Rather than a laundry list of rules and consequences, most of them spend time teaching what acceptable behavior is and how it manifests in the classroom, school environment, and broader community. What does respect look like in this classroom? How do you show respect to others and to yourself? How do you show respect for human rights and property? Intentional effort is made to build a sense of community that promotes positive relationship and interaction.

The value of building a positive classroom culture is touted strongly in the research related to classroom management (Marzano, 2003; Sylwester, 2000, 2003; Wong & Wong, 1998) and in publications on middle level teaching and young adolescent learning (Beamon, 1997, 2001; Jackson & Davis, 2000; Stevenson, 1998; Wormelli, 2003). An emotionally healthy classroom environment is one where relationships are good-natured and students and teachers interact with humor and optimism. Young adolescents feel protected and valued, and these supportive factors help to build self-esteem and positive self-concept.

Within positive classroom environments, young adolescents are also more apt to take risks academically. Neurological research indicates that in positive surroundings, students' brains release "feel good" chemicals that are beneficial to thinking and learning. Conversely, under emotionally negative conditions, students are "less likely to reason well, to grasp concepts, to understand relationships, or to make full use of the capacities associated with higher-level thinking" (Beamon, 2001, p. 54).

The three teachers in Chapter 7 are grouped together because of their purposeful efforts to create an explicitly positive classroom culture. Ms. Collis spends considerable time at the beginning of each elective eliciting students' ideas of indicators of positive classroom behaviors. The generated thoughts are handwritten on large colorful posters, labeled with the class section, and hung for visual reference. The Navigator Team of Haney and Bowes creates a classroom culture built around the five Ps of positive behavior. The way these appropriate actions manifest in the day-to-day life of the team is discussed and diagramed. Ms. DiLorenzo devotes considerable wall space to her No Putdown Zone. Respectful language and actions are the code of ethics for student interaction in her classroom throughout the academic year.

The "power of the positive" theme is reflected less explicitly though quite powerfully in the nature of teacher-student interactions, the use of the physical environment, and the quality of learning opportunities. Gardner (1999) observed that "students are more likely to learn, remember, and make subsequent use of those experiences with respect to which they had strong—and one hopes, positive—emotional reactions" (p. 77). Emotions that are activated by humiliation, sarcasm, high levels of frustration, stifled expression, limited relevance, continual failure, confusion, embarrassment, sense of powerlessness, or lack of resources have a counterproductive effect on thinking and learning (Jensen, 1998; Sprenger, 1999). In the classrooms in the preceding case studies, no teacher action or circumstance warrants negative emotion. Young adolescents are treated fairly and respectfully, genuine effort is made by the teachers to help all achieve, and students are engaged in meaningful learning experiences that encourage social interaction, choice, movement, and creativity.

In an earlier book (Beamon, 2001), I identified several specific practices supported by the brain research believed to engender positive emotions and interpersonal harmony in classrooms (Caine & Caine, 1997; Jensen, 1998; Sprenger, 1999; Sylwester, 1999, 2000, 2003; Wolfe, 1996). These include actions and activities (exercise and movement, constructive feedback, smile or affirming pat on shoulder, music, humor, laughter, handshake or high five, peer interaction) and instructional strategies (drama, role play, debate, games, simulations, cooperative learning, class discussion, journaling, problem solving, projects, celebrations, storytelling, peer editing, and interactive technology). These actions, activities, and strategies are gestures of support and encouragement that convey trust and acceptance of students as capable and likeable human beings. These practices are evident throughout the classroom management scenarios.

The pattern of the positive is further evident in the middle level teachers' intentional effort to cultivate open and honest relationships with the adolescent students. In each instance, they interact with students in a positive, courteous, and calm manner. This demeanor holds true whether in keeping students on task ("Mandy, is your hand raised to ask a question? If not, we need to move on"—Ms. Collis in Chapter 7) or in dealing with unacceptable behavior ("If I were to come over there, would you be working?"—Mr. Fox in Chapter 2; "I am not finished with class but I am stopping this activity because I am not pleased with your actions."—Ms. Wilson in Chapter 3). Expectations are clear and consistent, students are reminded why certain classroom standards prevail, and all of the adolescents are treated fairly. The teachers smile and laugh frequently and show genuine interest in students' families, extracurricular activities, and personal health. As Ms. Rickard in Chapter 3 expresses, "I try to be nice. Firm but nice, and they respond to that." The classrooms are positive and congenial places where students and teachers appear to like and respect each other and to not mind being there!

IN CONCLUSION

In a recent article in *Phi Delta Kappa* titled "Learning to Discipline" (Metzger, 2002), an experienced middle level teacher admitted that as a novice teacher she did not understand the difference between classroom discipline and classroom management. She openly describes her struggle as a first-year teacher who tried to do what she perceived as two different tasks: "controlling" a class of young adolescents and teaching a curriculum. Experience helped her to realize that proactive classroom management can facilitate instruction and student learning and eliminate the need for disciplinary action in most instances. While nothing works all the time and in every class, she ventures that "some environments, some teacher attitudes, some assignments generate more cooperation than others"—especially with adolescents (p. 80).

Chris Stevenson (1998), a prolific writer, veteran teacher, and staunch advocate for adolescent students, offers five guidelines for developmentally responsive teaching. He proposes that every young adolescent wants

1. To believe in himself or herself as a successful person

2. To be liked and respected

3. To do and learn things that are worthwhile

4. Physical exercise and freedom to move

5. For life to be just. (pp. 4–7)

The middle level teachers whose stories are shared in this book manage by creating classroom spaces where adolescents' emotions are engaged and their intellects are meaningfully challenged. They allow them to move, interact, and explore in a safe context of limitation, fairness, and consistency. They believe in their students and their potential for learning and self-discipline. Although each is mindful of personal style, strength, and tolerance, they collectively manage with trust, care, and appropriate expectation, and they are diligent in their effort to help young adolescents develop academically, socially, and personally.

Resource A

Collective Advice for New Teachers

Don't be too serious.

Be the adult.

Be firm and fair.

Be yourself.

Plan.

Network.

Experiment.

Ask for help.

Find a person/personality that you identify with and spend time watching how he or she keeps his or her classroom moving forward.

Talk with others, including your students, about issues.

Have a strong lesson plan and a backup plan.

Have clear rules. Enforce them.

Be consistent and keep trying different strategies until you find one that works for you!

Do not get pulled into petty, adversarial relationships with students.

Be interested in the students' lives.

Smile and tell a few corny jokes.

Do not tolerate any disrespect toward anyone in the classroom.

145

Resource B

Twenty of Our Best Recommendations for Classroom Management

1. Find out about students' out-of-school interests. Make positive calls home.

2. Make time to talk with students casually in the hallway or lunchroom.

3. Dislike the action, not the student. Rebuild after a negative exchange.

4. Engage students with a regular task or activity upon entering the room.

5. Write a daily agenda on the board. Have extra materials available.

6. Establish routines for classroom movement and use transition signals.

7. Plan for student collaboration, participation, involvement, and input.

8. Clarify common confusions to the entire class as a personal timesaver.

9. Give time frames for students to complete activities and adhere to them!

10. Give students directions *before* they move.

11. Use positive reinforcement and point out good behavior versus wrong.

12. Keep individual folders on students and involve them in their learning progress.

13. Have suggestions for students who finish early (brain teaser, book, magazine, puzzle, magazine, or special project).

14. Meet with students one-on-one to work out problems. Communicate frankly.

15. Smile, be nice, remain calm, listen, lighten up with humor, and laugh with them and at yourself. Don't take inappropriate actions personally.

16. Show your human side and don't be afraid to make a mistake.

17. Use individual homework planners for students and communication with parents.

18. Involve students in meaningful, challenging, and relevant learning.

19. Help all students feel welcomed and valued. Celebrate their uniqueness.

20. Focus and build on the positive. ENJOY these special kids!

Resource C

Teacher Profiles

School	Teacher	Subject	Grade	Race	Gender	Years
Eastern Guilford High	Heather DiLorenzo	English	9–12	White	F	7
Eastern Guilford Middle	Barry McDougald	Language Arts	8	Black	M	5
	Angela Morris	Art	6–8	Black	F	17
	Lisa Wilson	Language Arts	6	White	F	7
Hawfields Middle	Mike Armstrong	Language Arts	8	White	M	20
	Joyce Covington	Life Skills	6–8	White	F	27
	Heather Bowes	Language Arts Social Studies	7	White	F	8
	Jennifer Haney	Math/ Science	7	White	F	8
McDougle Middle	Patricia Berge	Science	8	Latino	F	3
	Erica Collis	Health/PE	6–8	White	F	2.5
	Priscilla Dennison	Science	6–7	White	F	15
New Hope Elementary	John Waszak	All Core	5	White	M	19
Turrentine Middle	Andrew Fox	Language Arts	8	White	M	8
	Melaine Rickard	Language Arts	8	White	F	10
	Jodi Hofberg	Math Science	6	White	F	13

Resource D

Featured Outstanding Teachers

Eastern Guilford High School,
Greensboro, North Carolina, Guilford County Schools

Dan Cunningham, Principal

Heather DiLorenzo, English, Grades 9–12

Eastern Guilford Middle School,
Greensboro, North Carolina, Guilford County Schools

Betty Parrott, Curriculum Facilitator

Barry McDougald, Language Arts, Grade 8

Angela Morris, Art, Grades 6–8

Lisa Wilson, Language Arts, Grade 6

Hawfields Middle School, Mebane,
North Carolina, Alamance-Burlington Schools

Clara Daniels, Principal

Michael Armstrong, Language Arts, Grade 8

Heather Bowes, Language Arts and Social Studies, Grade 7

Joyce Covington, Life Skills, Grades 6–8

Jennifer Haney, Math and Science, Grade 7

McDougle Middle School, Chapel Hill,
North Carolina, Chapel Hill-Carrboro Schools

Charley Stewart, Principal

Erica Collis, Health and Physical Education, Grades 6–8

Priscilla Dennison, Science, Grades 6–7

Patricia Berge, Science, Grade 8

New Hope Elementary, Chapel Hill, North Carolina, Orange County Schools

Barbara Chapman, Principal

John Waszak, Grade 5

Turrentine Middle School, Burlington, North Carolina, Alamance-Burlington Schools

Stephen Gainey, Principal

Andrew Fox, Language Arts, Grade 8

Melaine Rickard, Language Arts, Grade 8

Jodi Hofberg, Math and Science, Grade 6

References

Arnold, J. (2001). High expectations for all. In T. Erb (Ed.), *This we believe . . . and now we must act* (pp. 28–34). Westerville, OH: National Middle School Association.

Babbitt, N. (1975). *Tuck everlasting.* New York: Farrar, Straus & Giroux.

Bandura, A. (1993). Perceived self-efficacy in cognitive development and functioning. *Educational Psychologist, 18,* 117–148.

Beamon, G. W. (1997). Sparking the thinking of students, ages 10–14: Strategies for teachers. Thousand Oaks, CA: Corwin.

Beamon, G. W. (2001). *Teaching with adolescent learning in mind.* Arlington Heights, IL: SkyLight Professional Development.

Buehl, D. (2001). *Classroom strategies for interactive learning* (2nd ed.). Newark, DE: International Reading Association.

Burke, K. (2000). *What to do with the kid who . . . : Developing cooperation, self-discipline, and responsibility in the classroom* (2nd ed.). Arlington Heights, IL: SkyLight Professional Development.

Caine, R. N., & Caine, G. (1997). *Making connections: Teaching and the human brain* (Rev. ed.). Menlo Park, CA: Addison-Wesley.

Carnegie Council on Adolescent Development. (1989). *Turning points: Preparing American youth for the 21st century.* New York: Carnegie Corporation.

Chekhov, A. (1991). The ninny. In *Prentice Hall literature* (2nd ed., pp. 159–160). Englewood Cliffs, NJ: Prentice Hall.

Covey, S. (1999). *The 7 habits of highly effective teens.* New York: Simon & Schuster.

Cummings, C. (2000). *Winning strategies for classroom management.* Alexandria, VA: Association for Supervision and Curriculum Development.

Curwin, R. L., & Mendler, A. N. (1988). *Discipline with dignity.* Alexandria, VA: Association for Supervision and Curriculum Development.

Dahl, R. (1984). *Boy: Tales of childhood.* New York: Puffin.

Deci, E. L., & Ryan, R. M. (1998). Need satisfaction and the self-regulation of learning. *Learning and Individual Differences, 8*(3), 165–184.

Deiro, J. A. (1996). *Teaching with heart: Making healthy connections with students.* Thousand Oaks, CA: Corwin.

Dewey, J. (1938). *Experience and education.* New York: Macmillan.

Emmer, C. M., Evertson, E. T., & Worsham, M. E. (2003). Classroom management for elementary teachers (6th ed.). Boston: Allyn & Bacon.

Gardner, H. (1993). *Multiple intelligences: The theory in practice.* New York: Basic Books.

Gardner, H. (1999). *The disciplined mind: What all students should understand.* New York: Basic Books.

Geisel, T. S. (1957). *How the Grinch stole Christmas.* New York: Random House.

Glasser, W. (1992). *The quality school: Managing students without coercion* (2nd ed., expanded). New York: Harper Perennial.

Good, T. L., & Brophy, J. E. (2003). *Looking in classrooms* (6th ed.). Boston: Allyn & Bacon.

Gossen, D. C. (1996). *Restitution: Restructuring school discipline.* Chapel Hill, NC: New View Publications.

Hinton, S. E. (1967). *The outsiders.* New York: Dell.

Jackson, A., & Davis, G. (2000). *Turning points 2000: Educating adolescents for the 21st century.* New York: Teachers College Press.

Jensen, E. (1998). *Teaching with the brain in mind.* Alexandria, VA: Association for Supervision and Curriculum Development.

Keyes, D. (1959). *Flowers for Algernon.* New York: Harcourt, Brace & World.

Kohn, A. (1996). *Beyond discipline: From compliance to community.* Alexandria, VA: Association for Supervision and Curriculum Development.

Kohn, A. (1999). *Punished by rewards: The trouble with gold stars, incentive plans, A's, praise, and other bribes.* Boston: Houghton Mifflin.

Kounin, J. S. (1970). *Discipline and group management in classrooms.* New York: Holt, Rinehart & Winston.

Len, Bulgren, & Schumaker. (1994). The Unit Organizer © Len, Bulgren, & Schumaker. Retrieved from www.contentenhancement.org.

Lowery, L. (1993). *The giver.* New York: Dell Laurel-Leaf.

Marzano, R. J. (2003). *Classroom management that works: Research-based strategies for every teacher.* Alexandria, VA: Association for Supervision and Curriculum Development.

Maslow, A. (1998). *Maslow on management.* New York: John Wiley & Sons.

Metzger, M. (2002, September). Learning to discipline. *Phi Delta Kappa, 84*(1), 77–84.

Payne, M. J. (2001). A positive school climate. In T. Erb (Ed.), *This we believe . . . and now we must act* (pp. 56–62). Westerville, OH: National Middle School Association.

Paterson, K. (1977). *Bridge to Terabithia.* New York: HarperTrophy.

Perkins, D. (1992). *Smart minds: From training memories to educating minds.* New York: Free Press.

Philbrick, R. (1993). *Freak the mighty.* New York: Scholastic.

Rawls, W. (1961). *Where the red fern grows.* New York: Dell Laurel-Leaf.

Rivera, D. P., & Smith, D. D. (1997). *Teaching students with learning and behavioral problems* (3rd ed.). Upper Saddle River, NJ: Prentice Hall.

Rowling, J. K. (1997). *Harry Potter and the sorcerer's stone.* New York: Scholastic.

Sachar, L. (1998). *Holes.* New York: Scholastic.

Shakespeare, W. (1968). Romeo and Juliet. In G. B. Harrison (Ed.), *Shakespeare: The complete works* (pp. 474–510). New York: Harcourt, Brace & World.

Spinelli, J. (1997). *Crash.* New York: Random House.

Sprenger, M. (1999). *Learning and memory: The brain in action.* Alexandria, VA: Association for Supervision and Curriculum Development.

Stevenson, C. (1998). *Teaching ten to fourteen year olds* (2nd ed.). New York: Longman.

Sylwester, R. (1999). *A celebration of neurons: An educator's guide to the human brain.* Alexandria, VA: Association for Supervision and Curriculum Development.

Sylwester, R. (2000). *A biological brain in a cultural classroom: Applying biological research to classroom management.* Thousand Oaks, CA: Corwin.

Sylwester, R. (2003). *A biological brain in a cultural classroom: Enhancing cognitive and social development through collaborative classroom management* (2nd ed.). Thousand Oaks, CA: Corwin.

Taylor, T. (1969). *The cay.* New York: Random House.

Van Hoose, J., Strahan, D., & L'Esperance, M. (2001). *Promoting harmony: Young adolescent development and school practices.* Westerville, OH: National Middle School Association.

Wolfe, P. R. (1996). *Translating brain research into classroom practice.* Alexandria, VA: Association for Supervision and Curriculum Development.

Wong, H., & Wong, R. (1998). *The first days of school: How to be an effective teacher.* Mountain View, CA: Harry Wong.

Wormelli, R. (2003). *Day one and beyond: Practical matters for new middle level teachers.* Portland, ME: Stenhouse.

Index

Page references followed by *fig* indicates an illustrated figure.

**CORWIN
PRESS**

The Corwin Press logo—a raven striding across an open book—represents the union of courage and learning. Corwin Press is committed to improving education for all learners by publishing books and other professional development resources for those serving the field of K–12 education. By providing practical, hands-on materials, Corwin Press continues to carry out the promise of its motto: **"Helping Educators Do Their Work Better."**